AWAKEN, CHILDREN!

Dialogues With
Sri Sri Mata Amritanandamayi

VOLUME VII

SWAMI AMRITASWARUPANANDA

MATA AMRITANANDAMAYI CENTER
San Ramon, California

AWAKEN, CHILDREN!
Volume VII

PUBLISHED BY:
Mata Amritanandamayi Center
P.O. Box 613
San Ramon, CA 94583-0613
Tel: (510) 537-9417

FIRST PRINTING May 1995

ALSO AVAILABLE FROM:
Mata Amritanandamayi Mission Trust
Amritapuri P.O., Kollam Dt., Kerala
INDIA 690525

ISBN 1-879410-63-X

This Book Is Humbly Offered At The

LOTUS FEET OF HER HOLINESS
SRI SRI MATA AMRITANANDAMAYI

The Resplendent Luminary Immanent
In the Hearts Of All Beings

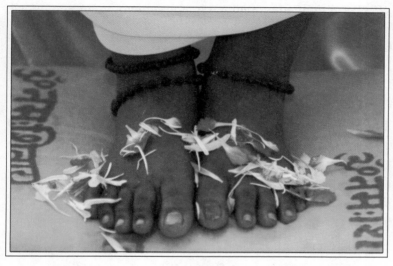

Vandeham-saccidānandam-bhāvātītam-jagatgurum |
Nityam-pūrnam-nirākāram-nirguṇam-svātmasamsthitam | |

I prostrate to the Universal Teacher, Who is Satchidananda (Pure
Being-Knowledge-Absolute Bliss), Who is beyond all differences,
Who is eternal, all-full, attributeless, formless and ever-centered in
the Self.

Saptasāgaraparyantam-tīrthasnānaphalam-tu-yat |
Gurupādapayōvindōḥ-sahasrāmśena-tatphalam | |

Whatever merit is acquired by one, through pilgrimages and
from bathing in the Sacred Waters extending to the seven seas,
cannot be equal to even one thousandth part of the merit derived from partaking the water with which the Guru's Feet are
washed.

GURU GITA
Verses 157, 87

CONTENTS

SONGS

PREFACE

To practice Vedanta in one's life is to dive deeply into real life, to know and experience life, in all its splendor and glory. Vedanta is not life negating; on the contrary, it is life affirming. It is part and parcel of life. It does not talk about something outside ourselves; it teaches us about ourselves, our true nature, our real existence. In fact, true life begins only when one starts exploring one's own inner Self. It is then that the real journey of our life begins. Mother says, "Just as we eat and sleep, the practice of spirituality should become an indispensable part of our life. Unless a balance is created between spirituality and materialism, true happiness will not be gained and life's goal will not be fulfilled. This balance is verily the core of life, and that indeed is the aim of Vedanta and all other true religions of the world." This book, the seventh volume of *Awaken Children*, is, I would say, the quintessence of *Vedanta*. It is a sure way to lead a most happy and successful life. Each word is profound and contains the whole of spirituality and life. Reading this book could be a meditation, a glimpse into one's own inner Self.

In every corner of the world we can find a number of people who are known as experts in their respective fields, delivering speeches and conducting workshops on how to lead a happy and successful life, on stress release, etc. This is a common occurrence in the modern age. Of course it is beneficial to a certain extent, but not in the long run. It will have a temporary effect on the participants, who will soon

fall back into their same old mental moods. Why? Because
the instructors, themselves, do not have the power to penetrate deep into the real cause of a problem and pull it out
entirely, along with its roots. Only a real Master, such as
Mother, can do this.

This is the age of fear and anxiety, the age of deep,
agonizing pain. How is one to get out of such pain? How
is one to reach the other shore of existence? How is one to
remain calm and peaceful in the midst of all the chaos and
confusion? Here is the way. Mother is showing us the way.
And not only that. She holds our hand and takes us to the
goal. What, then, is the secret? Mother tells us, "Be a witness and never move away from the real center of your existence. Dwell in the Self and simply watch everything as it
happens. Once you learn this art of witnessing, which is
your true nature, then everything becomes a beautiful and
most delightful play."

In Her dialogues with the disciples and devotees, Mother,
the embodiment of Supreme Truth, reveals, for the benefit
of Her children, several layers of knowledge. Illumined by
our beloved Mother's nectarous and gracious words the path
becomes very clear. We just have to walk this clear cut path.
Don't worry, there is nothing to fear, for Amma knows that
we are toddling children. And therefore, She is walking right
by our side, holding our hand tightly, helping and guiding
us with infinite love and compassion. Victory is ours.

Swami Amritaswarupananda
M.A. Math, Amritapuri
Quilon Dt., Kerala 690525
India

The events in this book, for the most part, took place between the beginning of October 1984 and January 1986. The exceptions are Mother's visit to the Meenakshi temple which took place in the middle of 1977, Her announcement about the end of Krishna Bhava which occurred in October 1983, and the death of the poet, Ottoor Unni Nambootiripadu which took place on the 25th of August 1989.

CHAPTER ONE

NOT THE LIMITED SELF
BUT THE INFINITE ATMAN

*H*ow is it possible for Mother to transform the lives of so many people, especially young people who have not yet enjoyed the pleasures of life? This is a question asked by many, both believers and nonbelievers. The answer is simple: When we are in Mother's presence and when we look into Her eyes, we are given a glimpse of our real Self. Mother's eyes reflect infinity. Her whole being gives us a glimpse of the state of being beyond the mind, the state of total egolessness. In Mother we behold our own purity, the purity of taintless love, the purity of the Self (Atman).

Suppose we have been eating junk food all our lives. Then one day we happen to eat a very nutritious meal for the first time, and it's delicious. Having tasted this delicious, wholesome meal, and if such food is readily available, will we still crave junk food? No, we will begin to crave good, nutritious food. Likewise, in Mother's presence, through Her every glance, touch, word and deed, we experience the ambrosia of immortality. We get a taste of it, and we sense that therein lies our real nature, the Atman. We also discover that what we have experienced up till now, in the name of enjoyment, is absolutely nothing compared to this blissful experience. It is our first exposure to the knowledge that we are not just the body, or small, limited self, but the all-powerful, infinite Self, or Atman (God). As Mother puts it, "We come to realize that we are not a meek lamb, but a mighty lion." Mother tells a story to illustrate this point.

"A hen once lay brooding on an eagle's egg which happened to be lying among its own eggs. After a period of time, the eggs hatched and the chicks came out. The eaglet grew up with the chickens, scratching and searching for worms in the soil. He was completely unaware of his true nature - that he was a mighty eagle. As the days and months went by, all the chickens developed into fully grown birds. But still, the eagle continued to live with the hens, believing himself to be one of them. He was completely deluded, identified with his existence as an ordinary farmyard cock. One day, another eagle who was soaring up in the sky happened to see our 'cock-eagle,' who was busy scratching and pecking worms with the group of hens. The eagle in the sky was amazed at what he saw. He decided to save Cock-Eagle by bringing him out of his delusion, and he waited for an opportunity to meet him. One day when Cock-Eagle happened to be alone, Sky-Eagle flew down and approached him. When Cock-Eagle saw the great eagle descend from the sky, he became very frightened and began to crow like a chicken. In no time, all the hens came running to Cock-Eagle to protect him. Thus, without

succeeding in his mission that day, Sky-Eagle had to
fly away. But soon thereafter, Cock-Eagle happened to
stray quite far from his friends and Sky-Eagle found
another opportunity to meet him. Slowly and cautiously
Sky-Eagle once again approached Cock-Eagle. This
time he managed to tell Cock-Eagle from a distance
that he was a friend and not a foe, and that he had
something very important to say to him. Cock-Eagle
was suspicious and tried to run away, but Sky-Eagle
succeeded in coaxing him back. He explained that Cock-
Eagle was not just an ordinary farmyard chicken, but
a mighty eagle like himself, who had the ability to soar
up in the sky. Sky-Eagle said, "You don't belong to the
earth. You belong to the vast, infinite sky. Come with
me, and experience the bliss of soaring through the air.
You can do it, because you are just like me - you have
the same powers that I have. Come on, try it!" In this
way, Sky-Eagle tried to persuade Cock-Eagle. At first
Cock-Eagle was full of disbelief. He even thought that
it might be a trap of some sort. But Sky-Eagle was
determined not to give up. Through his patience and
tactful manners he gradually managed to gain Cock-
Eagle's confidence, and then he asked Cock-Eagle to
follow him to a nearby lake. As Cock-Eagle had begun
to trust Sky-Eagle, he was feeling a bit more confident,
and he went with Sky-Eagle to the lake. They stood at
the edge of the water and Sky-Eagle said to Cock-Eagle,
"Now, look into the water. Look at your reflection and

see the close resemblance between the two of us." Cock-Eagle looked into the clear, still water. He looked and looked and he couldn't believe his eyes. It was the first time in his life that he had seen his own reflection, his real image. And now he knew that he didn't look like a chicken at all, but that he looked exactly like Sky-Eagle. After this experience his trust in Sky-Eagle increased tremendously. He gained a great deal of self-confidence and he unconditionally obeyed all the instructions given to him by Sky-Eagle. At first, Cock-Eagle had some difficulty in rising from the ground. But, not long after, the two eagles could be seen flying together, soaring through the sky with graceful majesty."

Mother says, "Most people are like Cock-Eagle, living their lives in ignorance without realizing their real abode." Mother reminds us, "Children, you are the all-powerful Self. The entire universe is yours. You are the Master of the universe - in fact, you are the universe. Don't think of yourselves as being meek, powerless or limited."

In Mother's presence we get a glimpse of our true nature. In Her we discover our real identity. We become silent and we gaze at Her with great wonder, for this is the first time in our lives that we have been given a real inkling of our true existence. When Mother says that we are not just our body, or the small self, the ego, but that we are the Supreme Self; Her words go straight to the heart because the words come directly from the highest Truth, the Supreme Atman Itself. She wins us over completely, and then slowly helps us to soar to the highest peaks of spirituality. We have been living like Cock-Eagle, not knowing who we truly are. And in the glory of Mother's presence, we come to know in a lightning flash that we are not of this world, but that we are the highest Self.

When we identify with the body, mind and intellect, we are living, like Cock-Eagle, in a state of delusion. We are mighty golden eagles who could soar up to the heights of the vast spiritual sky, and yet we live and die like chickens, without knowing our real nature.

CHAPTER TWO

THE MIND IS MAD

*M*other was chatting with the brahmacharins and a few householder devotees. A question was asked by one of the brahmacharins.

"Amma, if we truly are the Atman, why is it so difficult to experience the truth?"

Mother replied, "Truth is always the most difficult thing, and at the same time, the easiest. For ignorant and egoistic people, it is the most difficult thing to know, and for those who are inquisitive and have a burning desire to know, it is the easiest.

"People are intent on only feeding the ego. They never think of knowing the Self. To know the Self, one should starve the ego. But unfortunately, most people cannot starve the ego. Instead, they cling to it more and more. The predominant tendency in human beings is to attract as much attention as possible. They want to be praised and recognized, believing that it is their birth right. This is all food for the ego which thrives on attention. How are you going to know the Self if your ego is constantly craving attention?

"In order to realize the Atman, the mind has to dissolve. As long as there is a mind, you will be dominated by the ego.

"People point their finger at insane people and call them 'crazy.' But they don't know that they themselves are actually crazy, as well. Whoever has a mind is mad, because the mind is madness. In the case of a person who is insane, it is clearly manifested and therefore you can see it. Whereas, in your case, it is not so clearly manifested and therefore not as obvious. But the madness is there, because the mind is there.

"Look at people whenever they get excited, anxious or angry. They actually go mad. Anger is nothing but temporary madness, and it is the same with excitement and anxiety. When you are extremely angry you are crazy; you speak and act in a crazy way. It is a temporary state, in which you lose your mental balance. When such a state becomes permanent, it is called insanity. If you give in to your mind too much, and it is not kept under proper control, you lose your stability and go crazy. "The mind is the ego, which makes you very self-centered. But, instead of being self-centered, you should become centered in the Self (Atman), the real Center of your existence. For this to happen, the mind should be extinguished. The ego should die. Only then can you become established in the state of *sakshi bhava* (witness consciousness).

"The ego is the greatest obstacle on your path towards the Truth. The ego has no real existence of its own, for the mind and the ego are false.[1] At present we are under the impression that the mind and ego are our friends, but they are only misleading us, taking us away from our true nature. The mind and the ego have no power of their own; the source of their power is derived from the Atman, our real existence. The Atman is our true Master. But we are presently being controlled and misguided by false masters, namely, the mind and the ego. Not only do they delude us, they also cover the face of our real nature. Know this and try to come out of the limited shell of your mind and ego. The seedling cannot emerge and grow into a large tree unless the outer shell breaks and dies. Likewise, the inner Truth cannot be realized, unless the ego dies."

THE EGO LIVES ON ATTENTION

Question: "Amma, You said that the ego lives on attention. What do You mean by this?"

Mother: "Children, this is something we do every day, every moment. To crave attention is part of human nature. Whether we are conscious of it or not, all of us demand it. Human beings have an innate tendency to find ways through which to attract the attention of others. Even

---

[1] The mind has four different functions, or aspects. They are: The mind = the doubting faculty; *chitta* = The store house of memories; *buddhi* = the determining faculty; *ahamkara* = the ego - the feeling of 'I' and 'mine'. It is the same mind, but named differently according to its function.

a child wants attention. The mind and the ego cannot exist without getting it.

"A husband wants his wife's attention, and she wants his. Children crave the attention of their parents. Men seek the attention of women and women want to be noticed by men. People will do anything to get attention. The whole world is craving attention. This tendency also exists in animals. The only difference is that they have different ways of seeking it. Whoever has a mind and an ego is in need of attention and cannot exist without it.

"The things people do to get the attention of others are the same in almost all countries. It appears in a much grosser form in the teenagers of all nations. The things they will do to attract the attention of others, especially that of the opposite sex, are sometimes very foolish. But they do it, because at that age they are completely under the grip of their mind and ego. The mind is mad. What else but madness can emerge when you are completely under its sway? The product of a mad mind can only be madness.

"As you grow up, your mind and ego also grow, but they become more subtle and your ways of attracting attention will therefore also become more subtle. Your methods may not be as gross as before, but the craving is still there.

"Mother once heard this story.

"A journalist was writing an article about the mayor

of a certain town. The journalist wanted to know what people's opinions were about the mayor, so he interviewed a cross section of the town's population and asked them what they thought about the man. Everyone had something bad to say about the mayor. He was said to be heartless and corrupt; he was being blamed for everything that was wrong with their town, and there were many who said that they regretted that they had ever voted for him. He was a very unpopular mayor. Finally, the reporter met the mayor. The reporter asked him what kind of remuneration he received for his work. The mayor explained that he wasn't getting any salary at all. 'Then why are you so keen on retaining your position as the mayor of this town, when you do not earn anything and when you are so intensely disliked by the people?' asked the journalist. 'I will tell you why - but off the record,' said the mayor. 'I might be unpopular, but I enjoy all the honor and the attention that I'm given.'

"Many murders are committed just for the sake of getting attention. The ego reaches such a climax that a person may even think of getting recognition through acts of extreme cruelty. This is happening all over the world.

"A few weeks ago a young man came to visit Amma. He shamelessly disclosed to Amma that his greatest wish was to become famous. He told Amma that he had an intense desire to see his name and picture appear in a major newspaper. Amma talked to him for some time and tried to make him understand the folly of his attitude. In the end he changed his mind and regretted what he had said. He had simply been honest, and this is why he openly told Amma about his desire. But isn't this what most people long for? It's just that people are seldom sincere; they never say what they feel. There is a big wall between people, between the individual and society. People have lost their openness because of the predominance of their egos. They care only about pleasing their own minds and fulfilling their desires.

"When a child cries, it is asking for attention. All your ambitions and desires are based on the ego's strong yet subtle demand for attention. When you want to become a successful professional you are seeking attention. You don't want to be an ordinary human being, you want to be extraordinary, better than others. You cannot simply be content with what you are. You feel a need to be recognized and honored. This happens because people tend to dwell more in the mind than in the heart. Amma is not saying that you shouldn't have any such ambitions. It is all right to have them, but they shouldn't make you feel too proud and egoistic. You shouldn't get carried away by the mind and its desires.

"A scientist can be a better scientist if he learns to be less egoistic. A politician can set a better example and be an inspiration to people, if he learns to work more from his heart than from his mind. And a sportsman will achieve more if he is able to control his ego.

"The more egocentric you are, the more attention you demand, and you become too sensitive about everything. You expect people to speak and behave in a certain way towards you, and you demand respect from others, even though you may not deserve it.

"Amma knows a musician who demands to be treated with great respect. He is a talented musician, but his pride has made him an unattractive personality. One day, one of his admirers, who himself was highly musical, made a comment about the musician's way of singing a certain classical Indian song. The comment was made in front of a small group of the musician's admirers. Unfortunately, the musician couldn't take the criticism, even though it was put in a very mild, respectful way. He took it as an insult and slapped the man right in front of the others.

"Egoistic people, whoever they may be, are deeply afraid of not being respected. They are afraid of losing their importance. They cannot even dream of such a thing, because it is the whole foundation of their existence. Their ego feeds on the admiration and respect that they are shown by others, and if they don't get it they go to pieces. If people don't praise them, or show them the respect or the attention they demand, they become irritated and their tempers will flair. Because of their ego and their sense of self-importance, they cannot take any criticism, even if it happens to be construc-

tive. They feel deeply hurt if anyone questions anything about them. They always want to be the center
of any discussion, especially when they themselves are
present. Their whole lives revolve around whatever
attention they can get from others. When such people
eventually retire, their only source of entertainment will
be in recalling the past. They live in the past, because
that was the time when they were given the maximum
amount of attention. Their retirement will be a miserable experience, because now they have nothing to feed
their egos with, except their memories. They either dwell
on the past, or else, they keep some of their ardent
admirers very close to them, so that they will still be
given some attention and be told about their glorious
past.

"Listen to this interesting story.

"The period of final dissolution had come to an end
and the next creation was about to begin. Brahma, the
Creator, conceived a multitude of species. It was now
time to allocate to each species its respective life span.
He began with man. To man He gave a life span of
thirty years. But man was not content with that and
demanded a longer life. Brahma replied that a life span
cannot be arbitrarily increased, as the total number of
years given to all living creatures had already been established. But man insisted that he be given a longer
life. He prayed and pleaded with Brahma, until the Lord
finally said, 'Okay, let me see if I can help you. Stand

here beside me and wait. I am going to call the other creatures now. If any species do not want all of their apportioned life, I will let them decide how long they wish to live, and then I will give you the remaining years of their allotment.' Man gladly agreed and stood beside the Creator as He called each species.

"Brahma next called the ox and gave it a life span of forty years. The ox said, "O Lord, I couldn't bear to live such a long life. Have mercy upon me and cut it short by half." Brahma did so, and transferred the remaining twenty years of the ox's life to man. Man was happy to have a life that would last for fifty years.

"Next, Lord Brahma called the donkey to whom he allotted a life of fifty years. In a mournful tone the donkey said, 'O my Lord, don't be so cruel! It would be better not to have created me at all. My Lord, I don't want to live that long. Twenty-five years is more than enough for me. Please be so kind and give me no more than that.' Twenty-five more years were thus bestowed upon man. Thus man's life span had become seventy-five. But still he continued to wait expectantly.

"Following the donkey, Brahma called the dog and was about to bless him with thirty years of life, when the dog started howling in protest. The dog said to the Lord, 'No, no my Lord! I don't want to be on earth for more than fifteen years.' Thus man received another bonus of fifteen years.

"Brahma turned around to see if man was satisfied.

But lo! Still, only discontent was written on his face.

"The fifth species to be summoned was the worm. Brahma proposed for it a life of ten years. Hearing this, the worm almost fainted. It pleaded with the Creator, "O Lord, I shudder to think of such a long miserable life. Kindly reduce it to just a few days!" Again man was very happy to receive another ten years, which made his life span a full hundred years. Having been given the longevity of one hundred years, man rejoiced and danced gleefully in celebration, and he began to live his life on earth.

"Children, until the age of thirty, life is a period of education for man - a time when he is free from all worries and responsibilities of life, when he leads a carefree, easygoing life. Then he gets married. From then on, his life is verily like that of an ox. Just as the ox laboriously pulls a cart, man strains himself pulling the heavy cart of his family. In this way he reaches the age of fifty. Still he is carrying the heavy burden of the responsibilities of life and of his family. He no longer has the health and vigor that he enjoyed in his earlier days and he is also becoming lazy. His life, at this stage, can be likened to that of a donkey, for he is now living the life span of the donkey.

"When the years of the donkey have come to an end, man is totally exhausted and has lost his strength. For the next fifteen years, he is left to guard the house, like a dog, and look after the grandchildren. Most of his time is spent sitting by himself, or lying down, completely ignored by both his children and grand-children. He is now constantly thinking about the past, about old memories.

"The last ten years, which were borrowed from the worm, man spends crawling. Man is helpless, due to old age and sickness. His body and senses have become pow-erless. All he can do is lie down, brooding about the past which is all he has left. Finally, he passes out of this life, verily like a worm. The awful face of such a life is marked by despair, regret and misery.

As they were listening to this beautiful story, the devo-tees laughed softly as they recognized how true to life this is. Mother smiled at them and said, "Children, learn to live as if you have never existed. Only then will you live in Truth."

CHAPTER THREE

SAKSHI BHAVA
(THE STATE OF WITNESSING)

*T*he brahmacharins and a few Western devotees were sitting around Mother, at the edge of the Ashram grounds. One of the Westerners put forth a question about *sakshi bhava*, the experience of being a witness to everything.

Question: "Amma, the other day You were mentioning the state of *sakshi bhava*, or witness consciousness. I wonder if witnessing is a function of the mind, or is it an experience beyond the mind?"

Mother: "No, it is not a function of the mind. *Sakshi bhava* is a state in which you remain constantly detached and untouched, simply watching everything that happens, without the interference of the mind and its thoughts. You cannot be a witness to everything if there is a constant interference of the mind. The mind consists of thoughts. It can only think and doubt. In that supreme state of witnessing you constantly abide in your true nature.

"In *sakshi bhava* you become a witness to everything. You simply watch everything. There is no attachment or involvement. There is only watching. You will even witness your own thoughts. As you consciously observe your own thought process, you are not thinking - you are not doing anything. You are still. You are simply watching and enjoying, without being moved or affected by anything. How can the mind be in a state such as this? The mind can only think, doubt and cling. It cannot witness.

"The thinking process belongs to the mind; whereas, witnessing belongs to the higher Self. Witnessing is a state of abiding in Pure Consciousness. The mind and its thoughts are not real. They are the fiction of our own creation. Consciousness alone is real. Thinking may seem natural to you, but it is not natural. It is not part of your real existence. Your thoughts and your ego create nothing but restlessness and agitation. They don't belong to you, and you will continue to be restless until they are eliminated.

"Witnessing is the state of simply watching with perfect awareness. In the state of *sakshi bhava*, you are absolutely conscious. On the other hand, when you are identified with your mind and your thoughts, you are not conscious - you are far away from Pure Consciousness. You are in darkness and you cannot really see. The mind sees only the external world, the outer shape of things. It can never see something as it is, because you never see, you only think. And when you think, you miss the thing as it is.

"More and more accumulation and indulgence will only create more thoughts, and more thoughts will drive you away from your real center. In order to witness, one needs to be established in a supreme state of detachment. A clinging mind cannot witness; it can only be attached to thoughts and objects. It cares only about 'I' and 'mine.' In witnessing, there is no experience of 'I' or 'mine.' You go beyond all such limited, narrow thoughts.

THE REAL CENTER IS WITHIN

"When you become the witness of everything, you no longer have any claims. Everything, whether it be 'you' or 'I,' is the Supreme Lord, or Supreme Consciousness. Once you are established in that state, nothing can hurt or affect you. You move away from the mind and you are no longer identified with the body. The body is there, but it is as if it were dead. You don't give any importance to the outer world or to what people say. You know that you, in truth, cannot please or displease anyone. Sometimes you act as if you are crazy, at other times you appear to be an ordinary person. At one moment you may seem attached, and the next you are beyond all sense of attachment - completely carefree and detached. You may be extremely loving and compassionate, and then all of a sudden, you seem to lack any trace of love. Altogether there is something very unpredictable about you.

"Once you have attained the state of *sakshi bhava*, you can be in any mood you like, go to any level of consciousness - from the highest to the lowest and vice versa. But at the same time you are just a witness. Everything becomes a beautiful, delightful game - a wonderful play. Externally, people will still see you moving from one mood to another, from one place to another, and from one emotion to another; but internally you are motionless. You never move from that one center of Reality. The real center is within. It is not to be found in the external world.

"When you are established in that real center, you do not move. You are established there forever. And at the same time you can move without limit, in infinite ways, without ever leaving the center. You become God and God can move infinitely. There are no limits.

"Once you are established in the center of existence, you can ignore everything if you wish; or, if you want to smile at everything you are free to do so. If you don't want to sleep or eat at all, there is no need for it. On the other hand, you can eat what you like, and if you prefer to sleep for a whole year, that is also possible. But you will be awake within - wide awake. Though you may appear to be sleeping, you are not sleeping at all, and though you may appear to be eating, you are not eating anything. If you want to remain in your body, that is possible. Or, if you wish to leave your body, that, too, can be done. And, having left your body, whenever you wish to reenter the body, you can do so. Or, if you do not want to return to the body, you can remain where you are. You can choose the womb that you will enter and what type of body you will have. Anything is possible.

"People may say that you are doing something, but you know that you are not doing anything. You are just watching, just witnessing.

"So, witnessing happens only when you become totally detached from the mind and the thought process. You then become fully conscious of everything, even your own thought process. For the aspirant on the spiritual path this can also be practiced as an attitude towards everything."

BE FULLY CONSCIOUS

Question: "Amma, what do You mean by being conscious of your thought process?"

Mother: "Can you see a thought rising in your mind? Can you see how the thought works and how it dies? Once you are able to see a thought clearly, that very thought becomes impotent. Identification with a thought gives it power and the thought will then culminate into action. When you are not identified with a thought, it has no power. It becomes weak and inactive. When you see a thought and you are not identified with it, you are witnessing it. When you witness, you are fully conscious. In witnessing there is no thinking, which means that you do not identify with any thoughts. In witnessing there is only consciousness.

"You may see two people fighting with each other. As you witness their fight, you are not part of it, you have nothing to do with it. You are simply aware of it, consciously watching. When you witness, you are aware. You are wide awake. Your consciousness is unclouded, clear and untouched by what you see.

"But what about the people who are fighting? They are part of the fight. They cannot see because they are fast asleep. Negative energy and negative feelings such as anger, hatred and the need for revenge, cloud their minds and makes them blind. When negative energy is predominant, you are not really conscious, and therefore, you cannot witness.

"The mind consists of negative energy. Your thoughts are negative energy and your past is negative energy. To become a witness is to really wake up and become conscious of everything that happens, both within and without. But in reality, there is no within or without. In that state of supreme witnessing, you become the center of everything, just watching all the changes that occur. The changes never affect you because now you have become the center, the very life force of everything. In the state of witnessing you become one with the supreme, cosmic Energy."

Question: "Amma, You said that when we become the

witness, nothing will affect us. But, contrary to this statement, it is reported that even *Mahatmas* seem to suffer from physical ailments."

Mother: "Son, you are right. It is true that they seem to suffer, that is perfectly correct. They never suffer but they *seem* to suffer. Once you become the witness, you will witness even the death of your body, you will simply watch the suffering of your body.

"Listen to this story: There was once a saint who lived on the shores of the river Ganges. He was totally absorbed in the state of God-consciousness, and in that state he constantly uttered the mantra, 'Shivoham, Shivoham' (I am God, I am God). The constant chanting of the saint could be heard by the *sannyasins* who lived on the opposite shore. One day, as he was sitting on the banks of the river uttering the usual 'Shivoham, Shivoham,' a lion came down from the forests of the Himalayas and moved towards the saint. The *sannyasins* on the other side of the Ganges watched in horror as the wild animal approached the saint and was about to jump on him. They shouted across the river, 'Beware of the lion! Run for your life or jump into the water!' When the saint saw the lion coming towards him, he was not at all afraid. He accepted what was about to happen, for it was time for his life on earth to come to an end. And, as he was abiding in a state of oneness with all creation, he could not experience any difference or separation between the lion and himself. He and the lion were one, and it was he himself who was roaring through the lion. He sat where he was and continued to chant calmly, 'Shivoham, Shivoham.' The *sannyasins* watched as the lion sprung upon the old saint. As the lion caught hold of him, he continued without any fear to chant, 'Shivoham, Shivoham.' The beast began to tear at his body. But what a wonder! The saint continued chanting, 'Shivoham, Shivoham', as if he himself, in the form of a lion, was simply having his hunger satisfied. Throughout the scene of his death, the saint behaved as if nothing were happening to him.

"There are biscuits available in different animal forms. There are, for example, tiger and rabbit shaped biscuits. Do you believe that a tiger shaped biscuit is a tiger just because it has that particular shape? And when you see a rabbit biscuit and a tiger biscuit together, do you think that the rabbit has anything to fear from the tiger? Will the rabbit shaped biscuit feel frightened, thinking that it will be killed and eaten up by the tiger shaped biscuit? No, of course not, because, basically, there is no difference between them. The different shapes are made from exactly the same ingredients. It is the same when you know that your true nature is the Atman. You become a detached, impersonal witness, who watches everything in complete awareness, knowing that the different shapes of all phenomena, both living beings and every circumstance in life, are all made out of the same underlying ingredient - the Supreme Self.

"The mind is your past. Die to your past and you will suddenly become fully conscious. The past is nothing but dead debris. Get rid of it and you will learn how to witness. When you die to your past, to your thoughts and your memories, then you will be fully in the present. When you truly exist in the present, you are simply witnessing. The past can only exist as long as there are thoughts. When the thoughts are eliminated, the past disappears and you abide in your own Self. The Self does nothing but witness. The Self is not a person - it is Pure Awareness. It is completely detached from all phenomena. It is the state of being the one subject, the core of your existence.

"Children, at this time you are leading an unconscious life. You may wonder, 'How can I possibly be unconscious? I am walking, eating, and breathing, and yet Mother says that I am leading an unconscious life. Of course I am conscious! How else could all these things be happening within and around me?' You may have a hundred arguments to prove that you are conscious, but the truth remains that you are not.

"Son, you may say that you are wide awake, because you are walking, eating, breathing and seeing. Yes, you may be doing all these things, but, son, how many times a day are you really aware of your hands and legs, your tongue, your mouth or your breathing? Even when you eat, you are not aware of your hand that is feeding you, or the tongue in your mouth; when you walk, you are not at all conscious of your own legs - and are you breathing consciously? As you look around and observe, with your eyes, all the beauty and ugliness before you, are you aware of your own eyes? Even when your eyes are wide open, are you conscious of them? No, not at all. You are doing everything, but you are doing it unconsciously. You are leading an unconscious life. And yet you are eager to claim that you are conscious, that you are leading a conscious life. Therefore, wake up and be conscious."

Mother stopped talking and sat in meditation. After a little while She opened Her eyes and asked Br. Balu to sing a *kirtan*. He sang *Nirkkumilapol Nimishamatram...*

The entire creation rises and dissolves
within a moment like a bubble.
You cannot understand this phenomenon
unless the mind disappears.

The mind will vanish only when you realize
that the mind is an illusion.
You cannot comprehend your own mind;
it is enveloped by darkness.

The mind cannot understand the mind
for it conceals its own nature
But the mind will proclaim
that it knows.

You will come to understand
that the mind does not know anything
You will know
by keeping your mind calm and steady
and by doing tapas.

If you have really understood
then you will know
that the mind does not exist
that the mind is a no-mind
and once the mind is not,
everything shines forth as the Atman,
the Pure Self.

THE POWER TO WITNESS EXISTS WITHIN

When the song had come to an end, Mother continued to talk about witnessing.

"The experience of witnessing actually does occur in our day-to-day lives. It is just a question of being aware of it. And once that awareness comes, when you taste its flavor, its joy and bliss, you are on the right track.

"Say that a husband and wife are quarrelling. They are abusing and insulting each other, using the choicest of harsh words. Now, the couple from the house next door arrive on the scene. They could hear all the shouting and they have come to see what is going on. They do all they can to calm and console the quarrelling couple. But the couple continue to rage at each other. The neighbors talk to them and try to give them whatever advice they can. The neighbors are very calm and controlled as they try to handle this complex situation. They are able to see the problem and can therefore work on it. Finally, they manage to settle the dispute.

"How were they able to remain so calm and peaceful? Because they were only witnessing the scene, they were not part of it. Their minds were not as clouded or as turbulent as the minds of the quarrelling couple. They were much calmer and thus they were able to be good counsellors.

"On the other hand, the fighting couple were carried away by their turbulent minds and the dark, negative energy which they released. They were agitated and completely immersed in that darkness, both within and without. They couldn't see at all. They could not witness the situation because they were so completely identified with their negative minds. Whereas, the other couple were presently at peace with themselves, and were therefore able to gain a better view of the situation. Because there was some light in them, that is, they were not immersed in the situation, they could, to a much greater extent, stand back and just witness the event. They were not completely blind. The veil of agitated thoughts were far less present in them than in the other couple. But just the reverse would happen if they were to have an argument. Their neighbors who were now fighting, would, at that time, be able to stand back and witness, and it would then be their turn to act as counsellors.

"This example shows that the power to witness exists within everyone. It also makes it clear that witnessing is possible only if the mind is calm and quiet, only if you are detached.

"If this ability to witness can happen during certain moments of our lives, we should be able to experience it constantly, in any situation. This can be achieved because it is, in fact, our real nature.

"In the example given above, the mind still exists. It has slowed down at that particular moment, but the agitation will return. It is very difficult to be in a state of witnessing when difficult circumstances arise in our own lives.

"There are psychotherapists, counsellors and healers all over the world, who try to cure people's mental and physical problems. They may be experts in their fields, but they are professionals who are doing a job, and they are attached to it and to many other things. Witnessing cannot happen when you are attached. A person with many attachments cannot really help others. Only a person who knows the art of witnessing, who is established in the Self, in the real Center, can truly help others. The experts analyze the problems of their patients, which stem from the past, and they then try to suggest certain methods by which the patient's depression or anxiety can be overcome. As long as it is somebody else who needs the therapist's help, it is fine. He can help others to a limited extent. But what if something happens in his own personal life? Then everything collapses. The therapist is not able to apply the same methods to himself that he has tried on all his patients. Once something goes wrong in his own life, he cannot effectively counsel people anymore. He becomes useless. Why? Because as long as it is someone else who needs his help, the therapist can, to a certain extent, stand aside and observe the problem. His mind is comparatively unclouded and he just watches the other person's problem. The therapist is not involved in it, and therefore he is able to suggest some helpful methods. But when the problem happens in his own life, the mind exposes all of its negative tendencies. He can no longer be a witness, because he is himself entangled in the problem, completely identified with it.

"What is the use of all our methods if they cannot be applied to our own lives? And if they are not practiced in our own lives, how can they be expected to work effectively for others?

"Children, getting established in *sakshi bhava* is the real purpose of life. That supreme state of witnessing is the pivot around which all of life and the whole universe revolves. You may work, use your mind and your intellect; you may live in a house and have a family; you may have a lot of family responsibilities and you may have a lot of official duties to perform, but once you are established in *sakshi bhava*, in the real Center, you can do anything without moving even an inch out of that center.

"Being in the state of *sakshi bhava* does not mean that you will remain idle without taking care of your duties. You may be concerned about your children's studies, the health of your parents and your wife and so on, yet in the midst of all these external problems you remain a *sakshi*, a witness, to all that happens and to all that you do. Within, you are perfectly still and unperturbed.

"While enacting the role of a villain in a movie, the actor may be seen to be shooting his enemy, getting angry, being cruel and treacherous. But within himself, does the actor really become angry or cruel? Is he really committing those acts? No, he is not. He is just a witness to all that he does. He stands aside and watches without becoming involved or touched by it. He is not identified with the external expressions of his body. Likewise, one who is established in *sakshi bhava* remains untouched and unperturbed within, under all circumstances."

Question: "Amma, You say that a person who is established in the supreme state of *sakshi bhava* will be calm and unperturbed in all circumstances, whether positive or negative. But You also say that outwardly he may behave like an ordinary person. This sounds like a contradiction!"

Mother: A *sakshi* can choose. He can express emotions if he wants to, or he can remain unaffected. But such

people, even though they may outwardly express ordinary human feelings, will also possess an incomparable charm and beauty. There will be a natural charisma
about them. Even though they may express different
feelings, they can also switch off a feeling at any time
they want. If they choose to remain calm, quiet and
detached, they can easily do so. If they want to express
any feelings such as love and compassion in the extreme
sense, with their whole being, that, too, is possible."

Mother further elaborated, "Once you are realized,
if you outwardly wish to give the impression of being
affected by somebody, or an experience or situation, you
let it happen. Remember that you yourself allow something either to happen or not to happen, because your
mind, which is perfectly under your control, will not
receive, reject, or react to anything without your permission. If you want to remain still and detached as a
sakshi, it is possible for you to do so. But if you want to
set an example of renunciation, sacrifice and selfless love,
you simply live out those ideals. You may have to undergo
extreme sorrow and suffering, much more so than any
ordinary human being. But even then, you remain
unaffected internally.

"Suppose you want to express deep sympathy and
sorrow in front of someone. You know that if you do
this, it will create a great transformation in the person's
life. So you express that sadness. But you are just a
witness to the expression. As you are showing this feel-

ing of sorrow, the person in front of you feels grateful to you for sharing such feelings. Your deep love and concern has a great effect on him, because when you express a feeling you do it full justice, you express it perfectly and fully. You never express anything partially; your whole being is involved in it. Similarly, you can express any mood, at any time, whether it is positive or negative. Other people will feel it deeply and their hearts will be touched by it. It will invariably have the intended impact on the person. But the *Mahatma* is only a witness to the mood which is being expressed through his form.

"If the *Mahatma* wishes, he can express anger, anxiety, fear or excitement. But this will be only an outer appearance, because his mind will always remain calm and quiet. For him, it is just like wearing a mask. The *Mahatma* will wear different masks of anger, happiness, sorrow and fear, but he will do so for a certain purpose. And once that purpose has been served, he will remove the mask. He never becomes identified with it, because he knows that he is not the mask.

"Our problem is that we identify with all the moods of the mind. When we are angry we *become* anger. It is the same with fear, excitement, anxiety, sorrow and happiness. We become one with that emotion, whether it is positive or negative. We identify with the mask.

"When you are in a negative mood you may feel angry, and when you are in a relaxed mood you may feel peaceful and loving towards others. In reality, none of these moods are really you. For example: you have a house and a family, and a beautiful dog and cat. Suppose somebody asks you, 'Whose house is this?' What will you answer? You will say, 'It is my house.' And you will say the same about your car, family, cat and dog. They are all yours. But, whatever is yours is not really you. It is different from you. The house is yours but it's not you. Your body is yours but it's not you. It is the same with your mind, thoughts, feelings and intellect. They are yours but they are not you. You are the seer who sees through the eyes, you are the perceiver who feels the emotions, you are the thinker behind the thoughts; you are the one who feels, thinks, sees, hears and tastes. You are the experiencer, the subject. Once you become the very subject behind everything, all differences drop away and you go beyond.

"Not knowing that you are the power behind the entire universe, not realizing that you are its very life force, the totality of all existing energy, you identify with your mind, with its different thoughts and feelings, and you say, 'I am so and so - I am angry, thirsty, hungry, etc.' You identify with the outside, not with the inside. Once you are identified with the inside, then there is no longer any inside or outside, because you have transcended both.

"Throughout His life, from birth to the end of His incarnation on earth, Lord Krishna remained a pure witness to everything that happened in and around His life. The smile on His face never left Him, whether it was in the battle field or in the midst of dealing with any other of life's challenges. He remained perfectly calm with that alluring smile on His face. Even when Dwaraka, His abode, was swallowed by the sea, and when the hunter shot the fatal arrow which put an end to His mortal frame, Sri Krishna bore that same benign smile on His countenance, because He never wavered from that state of *sakshi bhava*. He was a constant witness to all that happened in His life. He never identified with the outside. He always remained as the Supreme Self."

Mother stopped talking and was suddenly in another world. Every now and then She would burst into a wave of blissful laughter. After a while She started making circles in the air with Her right hand. She opened Her eyes and requested that the brahmacharins sing a song. They sang *Parisuddha Snehattin...*

> *Your Name*
> *is the name of Pure Love*
> *You are the reflection of Eternal Truth*
> *You are the cool stream of peace*
> *that offers comfort to my heart.*
>
> *Your generosity is bounteous*
> *in fulfilling the desires*

of those who come to You
seeking worldly pleasures.

You pour out
the nectar of Knowledge
to those who surrender
at Your Feet.
You are the abode of peace and love
beckoning the soul.

You are spreading the message
of brotherhood
throughout the world
and You sing the song
of eternal freedom.

You are our inspiration
leading us to the land
of everlasting freedom.
You have lit the lamp of Love
and are constantly guiding us
toward the knowledge
of Eternal Truth.

At Your Lotus Feet
I place a flower
from the inner recesses of my heart,
with the prayer
that You will bestow upon me
the gift of undivided devotion
and steadfast yoga

*so that I may attain
the bliss of the Self.*

MOTHER, THE SARVASAKSHI

Mother is a living example of the supreme state of *sakshi bhava*. One only needs to observe Her life closely, to see that She constantly remains in that state. Her whole life serves as an example of this. Throughout Her childhood She had to undergo severe trials and tribulations from all directions. As She was living in the midst of people who were completely ignorant, She had to be immensely patient and detached to be able to accomplish all that She did. She stood firm and unshakable, like the Himalayas, before the tremendous difficulties that She had to face.

The *Bhagavad Gita* says,

Brahman, or the Atman, is uncleavable, incombustible, and neither wetted nor dried. It is eternal, all-pervading, stable, immovable and everlasting.

CHAPTER 2, VERSE 24

Mother could not be affected by anyone or anything. She never looked back and grieved, nor was She ever worried about the future. Calm and courageous, She managed to confront all the difficult situations in life with a smile, always ready to accept whatever happened. In the face of the never-ending suffering She went through, an ordinary person would have broken down, having lost all self-confidence and courage.

In spite of such adverse circumstances, of having no support from any direction, not even from Her own family, Mother managed to raise a great spiritual organization completely by Herself.

She was born as a village girl in a poor fishing community. She received no education whatsoever and had no money at Her disposal. And yet what unimaginable heights She has reached! How could this possibly be explained?

Somebody asked Mother recently, "What do You think about the enormous transformation that has happened to Your Ashram and the organization? There was a time when people tried to disgrace You and create all kinds of obstacles in Your life. But now You are recognized and worshipped all over the world. How do You feel about this?"

Mother smilingly replied, "Amma feels no difference of any kind. Amma is always the same. At the time, when the so-called difficulties existed, I lived within my Self, and now when so-called name and fame have come, I continue to live within my Self."

Yes, Mother is always the same, and Her love and compassion never waver. There is never any difference at all, and yet She can be playful and childlike when She wants. She can switch off from this world and dwell in Her own plane of consciousness whenever She feels like it. She can remain completely detached and can forego food and sleep for as long as She wishes. The world doesn't affect Her at all.

The ignorant villagers threatened Her life several times. They insulted Her and spread false rumors about Her. On one occasion, Her own elder brother, Subhagan, together with one of Her cousins, wanted to kill Her and even tried to stab Her. But even then, She could smile at them and say, "I am not afraid of death. You may kill this body, but the Self is immortal - indestructible. You cannot kill the Self." She then sat down calmly and quietly. But they were powerless. They couldn't do anything to Her. This is the power of the Self (Atman). And it is possible only for a person who is established in *sakshi bhava*, watching everything while dwelling in the supreme state of witness consciousness.

THE INFINITE POWER OF THE SELF

Mother once said, "Once you are established in the state of no-mind, no one can do anything to you, unless you consciously let them do it. You can allow something to happen or not to happen. Whether it happens or not, you remain a witness - completely untouched and unperturbed, ever established in the state of supreme detachment. Suppose someone wants to harm you or even kill you. They cannot lift a finger against you if you do not permit it. As long as your *sankalpa* (resolve) is not there, nothing they do can affect you. They will in some mysterious way always fail. Finally they might reach the conclusion that something, some divine power, is protecting you. But that power is the infinite power of the Self; it is not some power that comes from outside. The source of this power is within you. You become that infinite power. When you are egoless you are everything. The entire universe is with an en- lightened being. Even the animals, trees, mountains and rivers, and the sun and the moon and the stars are on the side of a Self-Realized soul - because in that state you are egoless. When you bow down before all of existence, in utter humility, the universe (existence) bows down to you and serves you. But, remember that you can also command them to turn against you, be- cause, either way, you are not affected.

"When there is no mind or ego, then you are one with the whole of existence, and the universe with all its beings are your friends. No creature will perceive you as an enemy. And even an enemy would be your friend, would be one with you, because your enemy is your own Self, though he or she would not be aware of this truth. If, internally, you are one with the enemy, strictly speaking, how then can he be your enemy? How can anyone or anything, sentient or insentient, that actually exists within you as a part of your Self, harm you in any way? It is impossible. Nothing can happen to you once you drop your ego, unless you want it to happen.

"The Rana of Mewar wanted to kill Mira Bai. He sent a cup of poison to her saying that it was a special drink that had been prepared for her, along with a beautiful and sweetly worded letter of apology for all the cruelty that he had shown her.

"Even though Mira knew that it was poison she nevertheless accepted the cup and drank from it. But nothing happened. The Rana tried to kill her by several other means, but all his attempts were in vain. As for Mira, she remained blissful and unperturbed throughout. How was this possible? Because she was egoless. She was beyond the mind.

"As far as Mira Bai was concerned, everything was her 'Giridhar,' her beloved Lord Krishna. She had no desires, because she did not want anything for herself. It didn't even matter to her whether Krishna loved her or not. All she wanted was to be able to love Him, claiming nothing for herself. For Mira Bai, everything was Krishna. 'Oh Lord! You, and You alone!' There was no 'I' at all, or any sense of doership. Her Lord, Krishna, did everything for her, whether it was good or bad. Whatever happened, she had no complaints. She simply accepted everything, seeing everything that came to her as His *prasad*. By surrendering to Krishna, Mira Bai surrendered to all of existence. For Mira Bai, Krishna was not just a limited person who she perceived only in that one particular form. For her, the entire universe was Krishna.

She had become one with all of creation. She had become one with the energy of Krishna. She was not aware of her own body. And when you do not have a body, how can you be killed? The whole of creation is on your side, protecting you. How, then, can any poison affect you? How can any part of creation harm you in any way? It can touch you only if it has your permission to do so. Only if you say yes will it affect you. If you say no, it turns around and moves away. Once you reach that highest state, nothing happens, even if the body is tortured or destroyed, because you are not the body - you are the Self.

"The entire universe is your body. Each part of creation is part of your universal body. When all is one, how can the part possibly harm the whole? How can the hand consciously hurt the eye? They may look different and their functions may be different, but they are one with the whole body.

"When you realize your oneness with the Self, the entire creation becomes your faithful servant. You are the master and everything in Nature is awaiting your orders. When all of Nature fully supports you, how can anything turn against you unless you really want it to? Nature will do whatever you command. If you say, 'No, don't do it,' nothing can happen. When you are in the right state of mind, nothing can harm you. Self-realization is the perfect state of existence."

This reminds us of an incident which happened in

Mother's own life. Mother once put Her hands into the mouth of a rabid dog. The dog had been one of Mother's early companions, at the time when She was living out in the open. Mother loved the dog very much, and when She saw that he had been chained to a tree, She went up to him and expressed Her love by embracing him and kissing his face. She tried to feed the dog and as She did so, She put Her hand into his mouth. Those who happened to be there and saw what was happening, were extremely shocked because Mother's hand was covered with the dog's saliva, which was highly infectious. They were all extremely worried and suggested that Mother take injections against rabies as a precaution. But Mother just smiled and replied, "Nothing will happen. Don't worry." And, of course, nothing happened.

Mother says, "Once you are realized, you become the cosmic Mind. All minds are yours. You become the sole controller of all minds, not only of human minds but of the entire cosmic Mind. This means that you hold the reins of every single mind in your hand. You have become everybody. Their bodies may be different, but you are abiding within each body. Your antagonist is nothing but you, yourself, in another wrapper. It is just like candies of the same flavor enclosed in different wrappers. The wrappers are of many different colors. They may be blue, green, red or yellow. The candies may think, 'I am blue, I am green,' and so forth. But what is inside? The same sweets with the same flavor, made of the same ingredients."

Mother once said, "All your thoughts and actions pass through Amma."

Infinite are the ways of a *Mahatma*. We are able to see only what we perceive on the outside. The *Mahatma* remains a total mystery to us - an unknown phenomena - that can be understood only when we come to know our own Self. We realize our limitations when we are in the presence of a *Mahatma*, whose infinite dimensions and unlimited love and compassion help us to feel humble. Only then will we become aware of our own nothingness. Only the feeling of nothingness and humility will help us reach the state of perfect fullness, the experience that 'I am everything.'

CHAPTER FOUR

A few new huts were being built for the brahmacharins in the Ashram. In the evening, after the *bhajan* singing, Mother wanted everyone to go to the seashore and carry sand, to fill the foundations of the new huts. As soon as this was announced, everybody went to the seashore with baskets and shovels. Mother led the way and soon the group arrived at the beach.

The night was dark and cool. The sea was rough. With a deep, vibrant sound that permeated the night, gigantic waves arose from the dark expanse of water and crashed against the shore. The sight of the vast ocean in the darkness of the night was awe inspiring and created a feeling of great inner peace. It also created a sense of openness and a deep awareness within the mind of all those present.

The sand *seva* (work) began. Everybody worked with great enthusiasm. Mother was also actively participating. Sometimes She used a shovel to fill the sacks with sand. At other times She carried a sack of sand on Her shoulders all the way to the Ashram. Even though the residents tried to stop Her from working, Mother wouldn't yield to their pleading. The sand *seva* went on for nearly two hours. It was now eleven o'clock. Mother sat down beside the ocean, surrounded by the residents and a few householder devotees.

Mother distributed salty banana chips and hot black coffee to all those who had been working. One by one, the brahmacharins and brahmacharinis went up to Mother to receive their share. As Mother distributed the chips and the coffee, She said to one brahmacharin who was standing in line, "No, you haven't worked, so you won't get any *prasad*. It is only for those who have been toiling hard for the last two hours."

When the brahmacharin left the line without a word, Amma's motherly affection overflowed and She called him back and said, "It's all right, son. Don't feel sad. Just carry one bag of sand to the Ashram and Amma will give you some *prasad* when you come back."

The brahmacharin did as Mother told him. While he was carrying a sack to the Ashram, Mother said, "He has to carry one sack, because Mother doesn't want to be unfair to those who have been working selflessly. Relaxation comes only after effort."

THE MIND IS A BIG LIE

While everybody was enjoying Mother's *prasad*, one of the brahmacharins asked, "Amma, yesterday when You were explaining about *sakshi bhava*, You said that the mind is unreal. I have also read that the world is unreal. Which statement is correct?"

Mother: "Son, both statements are correct. The mind is a big lie, and the world is a projection of that lie. Both are unreal. The world exists only because the mind exists. The mind is responsible for all your problems. It creates doubts and makes you suffer; it causes all your anger, hatred and jealousy; it prompts you to act indiscriminately and even to commit evil. It inevitably pushes you into a state of misery. The mind is hell. It is *maya* (illusion) and untruth. As long as you have a mind, your existence is unreal. Elimination of the mind alone can bring you back to the truth and to reality.

"The ego is a product of the mind. Therefore the ego is also a lie. It is unreal. Your existence will become full and perfect, only when you get rid of the mind and the ego."

Question: "Amma, You say that the mind and the ego are unreal, that the world of phenomena is only a projection of the mind, that our real nature is the Supreme Atman, or the Self. This is very difficult to understand, unless you can explain it in a much clearer way."

Mother: "Son, first of all, you must know that this cannot be explained in words. No matter how much proof and how many examples Mother may give, you will continue to have the same questions until you, yourself, experience the truth. The fact that the mind and the world are unreal is something which you, yourself, have to realize. Perform *tapas* (austerities) and you will come to know this.

"Children, know that the mind is the greatest mystery there is. But Pure Consciousness, or the Self, is not a mystery. Once you know the Self, you will realize that it is not a mystery at all - it is you - your own real nature. It is closer than the closest. The mind makes it a mystery. The mind is a complication which makes everything very complicated.

"You are not the mind. You are the Self (Atman). You are born within that consciousness. You grow within it. You live in it. And you die within that consciousness. But you are never conscious of this great truth. Why? Because of the mind and the world which is created by the mind. The mind makes it impossible to know the Self. The mind kills you; it dissipates all your energy and all your vitality. The mind is a thing of great weakness. Therefore, try to escape from that unreality. Get out of that great liar, the mind, the ego.

"Children, you always ask for proof and explanations. This is something that cannot be proven. Proof can be given of a scientific solution, and one can prove something which can be perceived by the senses. But the Atman is beyond science or any perception of the senses. You cannot prove it empirically. You experience it within you. But consider that it is the mind that is demanding the evidence. The mind which is unreal is demanding that reality be proven! The very source of your doubts and questions is itself unreal. All your doubts and your fears stem from that great liar, the mind.

"Here is an example. There was once a famous wrestler. No one could defeat him. He was unconquerable. He had been the champion of his country for several years. Being the strongest man in the country he naturally became proud and arrogant. It happened one day that a wrestler from another town came to challenge the champion. He accepted the challenge and a date was fixed for the match. Wide publicity was given about the great wrestling match which was about to take place. The fateful day arrived and the wrestlers appeared in the stadium. Our proud wrestler, the champion of the country, was very confident of his own victory. Compared to his opponent, he was stronger, extremely well built and had long years of experience. The fight began. The audience shouted and cheered for both of them, whistling and waving their hands. Some hailed the champion while others took the side of his opponent. The fight continued for quite some time. It was difficult to judge who would win. But finally, the visiting wrestler overwhelmingly defeated the champion, and the challenger was declared to be the champion of the year. The audience shouted, 'Victory to the new champion!', and they jeered at the defeated wrestler. They insulted him and laughed at him derisively. Somehow he managed to get up from the wrestling

mat and he walked away with his head bent in shame.
Long after he had left the stadium, he could still hear
the echo of the scornful jeers ringing in his ears. His
heart was full of hatred and his mind was very agitated. At this point he suddenly woke up.

"Yes, it had only been a dream! But our champion
was extremely restless. He had lost his peace of mind
and was walking to and fro in his room, like a caged
lion. His mind was filled with thoughts of revenge. He
was totally identified with the dream, and tried with
great intensity to figure out what method he would use
to defeat the opponent in his dream. He thought, 'Oh
my God! I have lost everything! I have lost my reputation. How can I show my face in public? From now on,
no one will respect me. How will I bear all their insults? I'd rather die than live like this. I'm going to seek
revenge against that idiot.' Such thoughts gushed into
his mind. Brooding and pulling at his hair, the proud
wrestler paced back and forth like one gone mad. But
the more agitated he became, the more he longed to get
out of his mental state. So, he eventually sat down and
tried to relax. And it worked. As his mind began to calm
down, his thoughts gradually subsided, and he soon
realized how stupid he had been. He thought, 'Oh my
God! What has happened to me? What a fool I am. It
was just a dream! It was not real at all, everything was
the creation of my own mind. I have been getting scared
and agitated about something that never happened.'

"Children, see how the champion was completely deluded by his own mind. He was totally identified with the dream and thought that everything that happened in the dream was real. Where did the other wrestler and the people, with their loud cheering and their insults, come from? Who created the different techniques that the two wrestlers tried on each other? Who created the stadium, the defeat of our champion, his shame, anger and desire for revenge? It was all created by the mind. Of course, it wasn't real, but still, the wrestler believed that it was real and reacted accordingly. As long as he was identified with the dream world created by his own mind, he had to suffer. But as soon as he realized that the dream wasn't real, he was released from its grip and found peace.

"In a similar manner, all of us are identified with a dream. The wrestler was identified with only a short dream. As soon as he woke up, the dream world disappeared, and as he relaxed, his identification with the dream also disappeared. Whereas, we are identified with a much longer dream. It is a dream that is projected by the mind, based on our thoughts and past experiences. At our present stage, we believe that the dream is real. We live in a dream created by the mind and we are identified with it. The awakening is yet to happen.

"You were asking for a clearer explanation. How can this be clarified as long as you are dreaming? The dream will disappear when you wake up. Only then will everything become clear. Children, you are all dreaming and you believe that the dream is real. No amount of explanations can make it clear to you. Until you wake up, and for as long as you identify with the dream, it will remain unclear. Wake up and you will realize that you were only dreaming, and then everything will become clearer than the clearest.

THE TWO POWERS OF THE MIND

"The mind has two powers: the veiling power and the power of projection. First, the mind veils the true nature of a phenomenon, and then it misinterprets it. That is why Amma says that the mind is a liar. It covers the truth and makes us mistake the truth for something else.

"A man was walking alone along a village path. It was getting dark, and he was struggling to find his way in the dim light. Suddenly, something bit him in the foot. He felt the area with his hand and discovered a small wound. He could also feel that it was bleeding. He suddenly froze when he saw a snake lying coiled in a bush next to him. He must have been bitten by the snake. The panic stricken man screamed at the top of his lungs, 'Help! I have been bitten by a poisonous snake! I'm going to die! Please, someone come and take me to a doctor!' The man was hysterical. He called and he called. He was now beginning to feel terribly tired and his head was spinning as if he were about to faint. He sat on the ground and continued to call for help. Within a few minutes, a man appeared out of the dark. He was carrying a torch. 'What is the matter? What happened?' he asked. 'I was bitten by a poisonous snake. I am dying. Can you take me to a doctor?' 'Don't worry. Of course I will help you. But where exactly did it happen?' asked the stranger. 'Right here, on this very spot,' replied the man. 'Look at that bush. There's a snake there!' The stranger turned his torch towards the bush, and what did he see? A thorn bush with a piece of rope entangled in it. The stranger said, 'Take a good look! It's a thorn bush. A thorn must have pricked your foot. The unfortunate thing was that you simultaneously saw the rope in the dim light and mistook it for a snake. Thus you were convinced that you had been bitten by a snake. But now that you know the truth, you can calm down.' Once the man realized the truth, all symptoms of tiredness and dizziness disappeared, and he began to relax.

"This is how the mind plays its tricks on us. In the above example, the mind first veiled the reality of the rope and then projected the snake onto it. The snake is your past. This is what the mind does constantly. The Atman, the one Reality, is veiled and, in its stead, the world of plurality is projected. The Atman (the Self) is veiled and our thoughts are projected onto it. This deceit of the mind goes on without end. The illusion can be removed only when a true Master brings you the light of true knowledge. Then you will realize the Truth and be at peace. That is when the real awakening takes place. Until then, the Truth will remain unclear."

WAKE UP AND YOU WILL KNOW

There was a short pause, after which another question was asked by Br. Venu.

Question: "Amma, the waking up that you just mentioned, and the state of *sakshi bhava*, are they one and the same thing, or are they different?"

Mother: "Son, both awakening and the state of *sakshi bhava* require being conscious. Real spirituality means to be fully conscious - they are one and the same. Most people are not conscious. They live in a world of non-awareness, for they are taught to live in this way.

"A child is born with pure consciousness, but society teaches him to be unconscious. The people who surround the child, his parents, siblings, friends and society, teach the child to pick up different habits. They raise him in a certain way, in a certain religion, with a certain culture, language, food, education, and habits. Everything around him conditions him. He becomes completely clouded and is made to forget his real nature. He is taught everything except how to simply abide in his real nature. Thus the child becomes unconscious as he grows up, clouded by all the conditioning which is forced upon him. He loses his purity and innocence, and he is never taught to be calm.

"In order to be conscious, one needs to be calm. Relaxation cannot take place unless you learn to break the shackles of the mind. The ancient saints and seers have, through the example of their own lives, shown us the technique through which to dissolve the mind, the thoughts and all the bondage that they create."

Venu interrupted and remarked excitedly, "Amma, why go so far back? You, Yourself, are showing us the right path."

Without paying any attention to the comment, Mother continued:

"Learn to be whatever you want in life, and at the same time learn this technique of being fully conscious under all circumstances. Once you have learned this art, you will always be aware and be a witness to whatever happens around you, without being involved in it.

"Suppose anger arises within you. Know that it is there. Know that the thought of anger has come up within you. When you are aware of it and can see it clearly, how can you become involved in a mood of that kind? Anger is a disaster. Nobody would consciously enter into such a state. It pollutes and poisons everyone and everything. Anger and all other negative moods of the mind are disastrous. They arise unconsciously. If you are conscious, fully awake and constantly watching, they cannot have any effect on you. Similarly, when an emotion leaves your mind, again, watch it consciously. At present, everything happens without our knowledge; we get carried away by all our thoughts and emotions, as if we are fast asleep within.

"*Sakshi bhava* can be both a practice and a permanent state. When you are permanently established in that state, then it will become spontaneous and completely natural to you. Witnessing will not happen unless you are ever wakeful. The dream world created by the past has no place in that state. The past must die. The mind has to dissolve, so that *sakshi bhava* can take place.

"Children, your true nature is like the sky, not the clouds. Your nature is like the ocean, not the waves. The sky is Pure Consciousness, and the ocean is Pure Consciousness. The sky simply witnesses the clouds. The ocean simply witnesses the waves. The clouds are not the sky. The waves are not the ocean. Clouds and waves come and go. The sky and the ocean remain as the substratum of the clouds' and the waves' existence. They have no existence of their own, they are unreal and constantly changing. Like the sky and the ocean, the Witness is the substratum. Everything happens within that supreme state of witnessing, but the Witness remains uninvolved. The Witness simply is - pure and untouched.

"In a similar way, the mind and its thoughts come and go. They are unreal and impermanent. They are like the ephemeral clouds of the sky and the waves of the ocean. They cannot touch your consciousness. Beyond the surface, your consciousness remains pure and untouched. That Pure Consciousness, which is eternally aware of all that happens, is the Witness, the *Sakshi*, of everything.

"To become established in *sakshi bhava* means to be ever conscious. Unless you are wide awake with perfect awareness, *sakshi bhava* cannot take place."

One of the visiting devotees said: "The *Lalita Asthottara* (108 names of the Divine Mother) says that Devi is the Witness of all three states of mind, namely: *jagrat* (the waking state), *swapna* (the dream state) and *sushupthi* (deep sleep). *Jagrat swapna sushupttinam - sakshi bhuttyai namah.*" The devotee joined his palms together and said, "O Amma, we believe that You are Lalita Parameswari, the Supreme *Sakshi*, who is the witness of all the three states of mind."

Mother began to sing a song, *Uyirayi Oliyayi...*

> *O Goddess Uma,*
> *Life, Light and Strength*
> *of the earth,*
> *where are You?*
> *O Wise One*
> *who is the wind, the sea and the fire,*
> *have You no mercy on me?*
>
> *You are the true, hidden Knowledge*
> *and in Your absence*
> *all the wisdom of the world*
> *has fled into the distance,*
> *rebirths are being endlessly repeated,*
> *unreality has become reality,*

and unrighteousness is increasing.
The monkey of the mind
wanders ceaselessly
holding the fruit of conceit in its hand.
Not reflecting on its real nature
it becomes food
for the God of Death.

After the song Mother was deeply absorbed in meditation. She was sitting completely still, immersed in Her own natural state of the Beyond. She seemed completely detached. The explanation She had just given about the highest state of consciousness had evidently removed the thin veil between Mother's real nature and the external world. Mother has said: "A thin veil has been created just for the purpose of being here in this world with all of you. However, this thin curtain can be removed any time that Amma wants to remove it."

Sitting in Mother's presence and observing Her, one sometimes experiences Her impersonal aspect, as well. At this particular moment, one could get a glimpse of this supreme state in Mother. Against the background of the immense ocean with its waves breaking against the moonlit shore, and the endless sky above filled with countless twinkling stars, Mother, in Her exalted spiritual mood, seemed an impregnable mystery. The entire atmosphere was permeated with a tangible spiritual energy, a unique sense of depth which in turn created an extraordinary feeling of peace within everyone. It was a moment of pure bliss. Almost fifteen minutes passed in this way. And even though a chill wind was blowing in from the ocean, no one even thought of moving an inch.

It was nearly twelve o'clock. There was a slight movement in Mother's body, and a few seconds later She returned to Her normal external consciousness. Everyone soon noticed that Mother had moved.

Some fishermen came out of their huts to see what was happening at this odd hour of the night, and a few of them even joined the group.

ATTACHMENT IS A DISEASE

Soon Mother could be heard speaking again. Mother said, "Human beings have two major problems. One of them arises when you do not get what you desire. The other problem is strange because it arises when you get what you desire.

Question: "Amma, that sounds strange! How can a problem develop when you get what you want?"

Mother: "Son, it is simple. Whenever your desires are fulfilled, that in itself will create a chain of problems, because of your attachment to what you have attained. And having attained the object of your desire, your next move will be to protect it, and your sense of possessiveness will only continue to increase. The mind becomes very turbulent, whether you get what you want or not.

In your struggle to safeguard whatever you have gained, you will lose your peace of mind. The real problem, then, is attachment, which is caused by the problematic mind. Attachment is a disease. If a person is too attached, it can even make him go insane.

"You cannot be attached to anything in the world and at the same time be at peace, because too much attachment to anything builds up a lot of tension in the mind, and this is bound to create pain. When you are too attached to anything, the excitement and anxiety born out of that attachment accelerates the thought process and intensifies the chaos of the mind. The pressure that builds up is such that your mind becomes uncontrollable. You don't know in which direction to turn, and you lose all sense of clarity. Your mind becomes like a forest after a cyclone. Until now, you could, to some degree, watch things from a distance as they occurred in your life. But now, the pressure of attachment has reached its peak, the burden has become too heavy, and you don't know what to do or how to face it.

"You lose your grip on life, and feeling utterly lonely and disappointed, you become an easy victim of your mind. You will drown in your thoughts; they will overwhelm you and swallow you up, as you become identified with the mind and all its negative emotions. An emotional breakdown takes place and you are forced into the darkest realms of the mind. You may even go mad. This is what our attachments can do to us.

"Mother will tell you a story that She has heard. A man was visiting a mental hospital where the doctor was a close friend of his. The doctor took him around and showed him the patients. In one cell a man was sitting on a chair, rocking back and forth while he happily repeated the name, 'Pumpum, Pumpum, Pumpum...,' over and over again. The visitor said to the doctor, 'Poor fellow. What is his problem? Who is this Pumpum?' The doctor replied, 'Pumpum was his beloved. She jilted him and ran away with another man, which is why he went insane.' The visitor sighed and went on to visit other patients. As they approached one cell, the visitor was surprised to see another man sitting in his cell hitting his head against the wall, as he uttered the same name, 'Pumpum, Pumpum, Pumpum...' The visitor asked the doctor, 'What is this? Has Pumpum something to do with this man, too?' The doctor replied, 'Yes, this is the man who Pumpum finally married.'"

There was uproarious laughter as Mother finished the story. In the stillness of the night, it sounded like an explosion. The laughter slowly subsided and merged with the sound of the ocean. At about twelve-thirty a.m. Mother got up and, followed by Her children, She returned to the Ashram.

It had been a wonderful night. These are unforgettable events which create a deep impression in the heart of the disciple - invaluable events upon which there is so much to contemplate. Living with a true, living Master is a rare blessing, the rarest and most precious blessing a human being can receive. These moments will later create endless waves of intense love and longing in the disciple, which will finally cause him to dive deep into his own consciousness and thereby soar to the heights of spiritual bliss. Blessed indeed are the ones who associate with a great Master like Mother.

WHEN AMMA SAYS, "DON'T WORRY..."

One devotee was saying, "When Amma says, 'Don't worry,' there is no point in worrying, because somehow or other the problem will be sorted out."

This is the experience of many devotees. The devotee who made the comment had come this evening with his whole family to see Mother and to receive Her blessings. He had a special reason for saying this.

A year and a half ago, his daughter had been given away in marriage to a pious young man, and the couple had begun a very happy married life together. A few months after the wedding, to the family's great shock, the young woman was diagnosed with cancer of the womb. She was five months pregnant at the time. The doctors were of the opinion that it was a serious, extremely complicated case. There was a tumor in the womb which was thought to be malignant and it had to be removed through surgery. The doctors were pessimistic about the outcome of the operation. They didn't believe that the baby would survive, and the mother's chances of survival were also very slim. The doctors actually told the parents of the young woman that God alone could save their daughter and the baby. The worried parents went to Mother, their only source of hope. They told Her about their daughter's life-threatening illness and prayed for Her Grace. The whole family had been very devoted to Mother, ever since they first met Her in 1981. Whenever they had a problem they always turned to Mother for Her Grace and guidance.

Mother listened to their problem, and, having expressed Her deep concern for their daughter, She said to them, "Don't worry. Mother will take care of both your daughter and the baby." They had complete faith in Mother, and after She said this they didn't worry anymore, even though, four months later, the girl still had to undergo the operation. Their faith in Mother's words proved to be one hundred percent correct. The operation was performed, the baby was removed from the womb, and to the wonderment of the doctors, both mother and child survived. The doctors removed a tumor weighing four pounds from her womb. And even though the doctors still expected complications to set in, there were no complications at all; everything went smoothly. Both mother and baby were perfectly healthy.

When Mother came down from Her room, the family, who were anxiously waiting to receive Her *darshan*, came rushing up to Her. They prostrated before Her and placed the newborn babe at Her feet. Through tears of gratitude, the mother of the baby said to Mother, "Amma, he was born only because of Your Grace." Mother picked up the infant, and as She held him in Her arms and was fondling him, She said, "See how much trouble you have caused your mother, just for her to give birth to you!"

Mother sat down at the bottom of Her staircase. Soon She was surrounded by the Ashram residents. The baby kept looking at Mother, gazing intently at Her face. He had a dark complexion and because of this, Mother called him 'Karumba' (The black one). Mother continued, "Son, you are black just like Amma. Don't you want to be fair like your mother?" The baby suddenly began to cry. Mother said, "It seems that he didn't like it that Amma called him Karumba."

The baby's grandfather was bursting with excitement and couldn't contain himself anymore. "No! No!" he retorted, "He was very happy when you called him 'The black one.' He rejoiced to hear that he is as dark as You, Amma. But he didn't like it when You asked if he wanted to be fair like his mother. He is protesting! That is why he's crying!"

Everyone was delighted by this sweet remark and laughed in appreciation. Mother also joined in the laughter, as She returned the baby to its mother.

THE NECESSITY OF TAPAS

Mother turned to the residents who were sitting next to Her and said: "Immense *tapas* (austerities) is needed for any new birth to take place. Take, for example, the birth of a child. A mother is literally doing *tapas* during her pregnancy. She has to be very careful with everything she does, the way she moves and acts, and even in the way in which she's lying down. She cannot eat certain foods, and she must not strain herself by doing too much physical work. She may have to avoid certain kinds of situations where she could get nervous or upset, and it wouldn't be good for her to brood over things or be anxious. Only if the mother follows all the instructions given by her doctor will she give birth to a healthy, intelligent child. If she makes a mistake it could harm the baby. The pregnant woman will constantly be thinking about the child she is carrying in her womb. She will never forget the baby for a moment and her awareness will be tremendous. Similarly, we ourselves should have the same commitment to the spiritual birth that is about to take place in us. This commitment is known as *tapas*.

"For anything to be born, whether it be, for example, the birth of a nation, an institution or a business, it requires a lot of *tapas*. Only through *tapas* can one attain the heights of any chosen field; it doesn't matter which. Whether you are a spiritual person or a person whose aims are predominately material, if you want to become a real master in your field, it is absolutely necessary to do *tapas*.

"To seek spiritual attainment is to die and to be born again. The ego needs to die. Only then can the real you be born. And just like any birth process, you will have to undergo *tapas*, intense *tapas*. *Tapas* is, in a way, unavoidable; it is the pain which you have to undergo in the process of gaining anything. In order to reach the spiritual goal, a maximum amount of *tapas* is needed. The difference between the spiritual goal and other aspirations lies only in degree. Spiritual realization is the highest type of happiness that can be attained, and therefore, the price that you have to pay for it is also very high.

"It's just common sense. The happiness that we gain from the outer world is fleeting; it never stays with you for long. It is there for one moment and the next moment it is gone. But, spiritual bliss is not like that. Once the final breakthrough happens, that is, once you transcend the limitations of body, mind and intellect, once you reach that state, there is no return. The bliss is forever. And it is infinite. But for this to happen you need to pay accordingly. It is not sufficient to pay with only a part of yourself, you have to pay with everything. Your entire life is what has to be given.

"You have to sacrifice a great deal just to gain a few material objects, or to attain a higher position, or to become famous. You need to study and train yourself to gain a fitting education and whatever qualifications you may need. Many people sacrifice the pleasures of family life to attain a higher position in society, or to acquire a more profitable business. A lot of time and energy have to be concentrated towards that end. The more happiness you want to enjoy, the more effort is necessary, and the more you have to pay.

However much you grow materially, the pain and tension will remain with you. It doesn't end. Whereas, in spirituality, once you attain the highest peak, all pain and tension disappear. You will become completely independent and fully relaxed.

"If, on the other hand, you wish to remain in your own village, content with your modest work and enjoy the pleasure of being with your family, that is fine. It will be less strenuous and will consume much less of your time and energy. The *tapas* or pain that you have to undergo will be relatively small. But if you are very ambitious and wish to earn more money, believing that this will make you happier, then you will have to do much more *tapas*. However, if you desire to become a doctor or a scientist in a foreign country, such as the United States of America, then the intensity of the *tapas* (commitment) or pain required will be very great.

"So, if a person wants to become the happiest person in the world, the only way to gain the highest type of happiness is to lead a spiritual life, performing intense *tapas*. This is simple logic. Just to become the owner of a few things - a house, a car, or a plot of land - you have to pay a great deal and a lot of sacrifice is involved. But spirituality is like becoming the owner of the entire universe. The universe becomes yours; it becomes your servant and you become the master. You can imagine the amount of *tapas* you will have to do to own the universe, to become that wealthy, to become the Lord of the Universe, to be the happiest of all, for all times to come.

"Yes, children, it is a new birth. To become truly spiritual, you need to be born again. And only if you die will the real You be born.

"As the outer shell of the seed dies, the seedling emerges. Gradually it grows into a shady tree with an abundance of fruits and flowers. Likewise, the outer shell, the body and the ego, should die so that we may grow into the Atman (the Self).

"Just as a mother is willing to endure the pain of giving birth to a child, a true *sadhak* (spiritual aspirant) should be willing to undergo the pain of *tapas* with great perseverance and immense awareness, so that he can blossom into a divine, beautiful and fragrant flower. The bud opens for the flower to unfold, and as the bud breaks open, some pain is involved. At this stage, your heart is like a bud, and in order for your heart to open, the pain and the heat of *tapas* are unavoidable. *Tapas* literally means heat. Only the heat produced by *tapas*, the pain and the longing that it creates, can burn up the mind along with all its thoughts, its *vasanas* (tendencies) and the ego. The process of opening is painful, but once it opens up, the beauty and charm of the divine flower of the heart is indescribable and eternal."

BE AN INNOCENT BEGINNER

Question: "What is the best way for this opening to happen?"

Mother: "Son, can you remain a beginner forever? If you can remain an innocent beginner, that is the best way for this opening up to happen."

One brahmacharin exclaimed, "Beginner! What do you mean by that, Amma?"

Mother: "Yes, son, only when you are aware of your ignorance can you remain with the attitude of a beginner. A beginner is always ignorant and he knows that he is ignorant. Therefore, he listens intently. He is open and receptive. Once you think that you know, then you do not listen anymore; you only speak. Your mind and intellect become full. You are not a beginner anymore, you have turned into a knowledgeable person. But in reality, a knowledgeable person is more ignorant than others, because he is completely closed. He has lost his ability to be open and receptive. He may be knowledgeable, but he does not really know. To really know is different from being knowledgeable. You need to be open in order to know. You need to be an innocent beginner.

"The beginner is able to bow down in humility, and because of this, true knowledge flows into him. But a knowledgeable person is merely full of information and tends to be egoistic. He therefore cannot bow down and be humble. True knowledge cannot enter into him. There is no room for it and so it spills out.

"Amma has a story to tell you. A *Mahatma* once lived in a deep forest. One day, a very scholarly person came to the forest to visit him. The scholar was in a great hurry and said to the *Mahatma*, 'Revered Sir, can you tell me something about meditation?' The *Mahatma* smiled at him and said, 'Why are you in such a hurry? Sit down, relax and have a cup of tea. Then we will discuss the matter, there is time enough.' But the scholar was very restless and impatient. He said, 'Why can't we do it right now? Tell me something about meditation!' However, the *Mahatma* insisted that the scholar should sit down, relax and have a cup of tea before he would talk to him. Finally, the scholar had to yield to the *Mahatma* and he sat down. But, as is the nature of a scholar, he couldn't possibly relax. He was constantly talking within. The *Mahatma* took his own time. He made the tea and came back to the scholar who was waiting for him impatiently. The *Mahatma* handed a cup and a saucer to the scholar and then he began to pour the tea into the cup. The cup became full, it started to overflow, but the *Mahatma* did not stop pouring. The scholar shouted, 'What are you doing? The cup is full!

Stop pouring!' But the *Mahatma* kept on pouring. The tea overflowed into the saucer and from the saucer it slowly began to drip onto the floor. The scholar shouted at the top of his voice, 'Hey, are you blind! Can't you see that the cup is full and that it cannot contain another drop?' The *Mahatma* smiled and stopped pouring the tea. 'That is right,' he said. 'The cup is full and it cannot contain another drop. So, you know that when a cup is full it cannot contain any more. How then can you, who are brimful with information, listen to me when I talk about meditation? It's impossible. So, first empty your mind and then I will talk to you. However, meditation is an experience; it cannot be explained verbally. Meditation happens only when you get rid of your mind and your thoughts.' "

Mother continued, "Knowledgeable people or intellectuals only know how to talk. They cannot listen. Listening is possible only when you are empty within. Only one who has the attitude, 'I am a beginner, I am ignorant,' can listen with faith and love. Others cannot listen.

"If you observe two scholars talking to each other, you will see that neither of them is listening to what the other is saying. But you will also see that one is keeping quiet while the other is talking and vice versa. You may think that they are listening to each other, but, in fact, they are not. They cannot listen. When one speaks, the other one may not be speaking externally, but he is speaking within, forming his own ideas and interpretations. Each one is waiting for the other to stop so that he can start, and there will be no connection between what they are saying to each other. One will be talking about A and the other will be talking about Z. Neither of them is a good listener; they each know only how to speak.

HOW TO LISTEN

"If you want to be a good disciple, you must become a good listener, a listener endowed with faith and love. You must always have the attitude of being a beginner, so that you can listen properly. Such a beginner will be completely open and innocent, like a child."

Question: "Amma, I feel that I do listen when You talk. I don't think that I am talking to myself when You are speaking. Or am I?"

Mother: "Son, Amma is not saying that you aren't listening. You are listening, but only partially. You listen with your mind. Your listening is divided, not undivided.

"If you, for example, look at the people who are watching a cricket match or a football match, you will see that they sometimes forget themselves. When their favorite player bowls or kicks the ball, they will also make funny movements with their hands or legs, and sometimes you will see some odd expressions on their faces. They are participating with their bodies. But they do not forget themselves completely; they are still there, engrossed in the play, but only partially.

"When a great musician is performing, the listeners will participate, shaking their heads and clapping their hands. But this is only partial participation, only emotional participation. Your whole being is not involved.

"When you listen to a song, you are present; whereas, in actual participation, you are completely absent. You forget yourself. Your whole being, every cell of your body, opens up and you receive wholly, without missing a single drop. As you drink in the object of your thoughts or meditation, you become one with it. In that kind of participation you yourself are totally absent. It is as if the player is absent - only the play exists. The singer is absent - only the song exists.

"When Mira Bai sang and danced, her whole being participated. When the *gopis* of Vrindavan longed to see Krishna, their whole being participated. They forgot themselves. They became identified with Krishna.

"Your listening becomes complete only when your whole being participates. Only then will true knowledge flow into you. When you learn to listen to the Master with your whole being, then you yourself are absent. You cannot be present; your mind or ego cannot remain present in that kind of listening or participation. You identify with your Master, with his infinite consciousness, and you become everything.

"Once, Lord Krishna and Arjuna went for a stroll. They had a long, pleasant talk. At one point Krishna said to Arjuna, 'You say that you believe that I am an incarnation of God. Then, come with Me, for today there is something that I want to show you.' They walked together along the countryside. After a while, Krishna stopped and pointed at a large vine bush growing in a field, and He said, 'What do you see there?' Arjuna replied, 'I see a huge vine, bearing clusters of ripe grapes.' The Lord said, 'You are mistaken, Arjuna. That is not a vine and those are not grapes. Take a closer look.' Arjuna looked again at the vine and was amazed to find that before him there was no vine at all. There was only the Lord. And there were no bunches of grapes, only countless forms of Krishna hanging from the form of Krishna.

"When you participate wholly, you become everything, you identify with the entire universe. A new world opens up before you, and you become permanently established in that state.

THE THREE TYPES OF STUDENTS

"The scriptures talk about three types of students. The best, most competent student listens to the Master's words with his whole being. If the Master tells him, 'You are Brahman,' He immediately realizes Brahman, the Absolute Reality. How does this happen? Because he listens totally - his whole being participates in that listening. He listens with undivided faith and unconditional love. Such a student must have an unquenchable thirst to know. He drinks in his Master's words - nay, he drinks in the Master, Himself, with his whole being. The saying, 'You are Brahman,' goes straight into his heart and he realizes.

"Such a disciple maintains the attitude of a beginner, an innocent beginner. He may have learned all the scriptures but he still remains a beginner, innocent as a child. He is extremely humble and therefore, true knowledge flows into him. The deepest knowledge is available only when you learn how to participate with your whole being, only when you learn the art of bowing down before all of creation in utter humility.

"The second type of disciple listens, but only partially. It will take much more time for him to realize the truth. He does listen, but only emotionally - he does not listen totally. His listening is divided; his faith and love are divided. The Master, therefore, has to be very patient with him, so that he may learn how to listen fully. He doesn't yet know the art of forgetting everything and participating with his whole being. True knowledge can enter into him only when he listens to the Master with such intensity that he forgets himself. The ever vacillating and doubtful mind will not allow him to be an innocent beginner, so that the knowledge may flow into him. He sometimes manages to do it, but before long the mind comes back. The receptivity comes and goes. The mind does not allow him to remain firmly in that state. The mind shouldn't interfere at all. It shouldn't ask any questions. Only then does the mind cease to interfere and total listening becomes possible. Until then the disciple will listen only partially. But a true Master, who is patience and compassion embodied, will help him to reach the final goal.

"The third type is the disciple who is intellectually inclined. He is very talkative within, and his mind contains so much information that he cannot listen at all. Such a disciple will be very egocentric, and the attitude of 'I' and 'mine' will be very predominant in him. The Master has to wait with endless patience to bring him to the light. The disciple's ability to listen is extremely poor, because he does not know how to be an innocent beginner at all. He cannot bow down and be humble, and therefore, true knowledge will not flow into him. Even if the Master constantly repeats to him, 'You are God. You are God... You are Brahman, the Absolute,' the disciple will constantly be asking within, 'How?' 'Why?' 'What?' 'When?' *ad infinitum*, because his intellect is crammed with his own ideas and those of the scriptures. The Master must have tremendous patience to bring this kind of disciple to the right track. The divine discus alone can open up a crack in such a disciple. The true Master will finally use the divine discus of true knowledge to break open the ego of the disciple. He will empty his intellect by making him feel the heavy burden of his storehouse of limited knowledge, and he will then fill the disciple's heart with true knowledge and with the light and love of God. This is a tremendous job which can only be done by a true Master."

Mother is a living example of someone who does everything with Her whole being. Her entire being participates during *darshan*, when She speaks and sings *bhajans*, and when She works with everyone in the Ashram. Mother participates fully and completely in whatever She is doing at the moment. While receiving Her children during *darshan*, Mother offers Herself to them and forgets Herself. Mother doesn't care about Her own body or any physical comforts. She is completely available to Her devotees, offering them Her whole being as She participates in their happiness and sorrow, their success and failures. She is fully present without the least presence of an ego or any judgement.

In whatever Mother does, Her whole being participates. She is totally in the present. We see only Her outer form, but She is not there. Pure Being alone exists. Her presence and participation is total, and it is deeply inspiring. Mother cannot do anything halfheartedly. She can only participate in Her fullness. It is this fullness that makes Mother's presence such a wonderful and unforgettable experience in one's life. And it is this fullness that adds a special charm and beauty to all that She does. It becomes a meditation. Mother's smile, the way She walks, Her voice, Her glance and Her touch, every detail of what Mother does is so perfect, because She is *Purnam*. She is the Whole.

CHAPTER FIVE

*M*other was in Calicut for a few days. It was Her first visit to that part of the state. She was staying in the home of a devotee. The morning *darshan*s were also held at the house. There was a constant flow of devotees who came each day to receive Mother's *darshan*.

Mother was sitting on a cot in Her room, which was quite big, and She was receiving the devotees, one by one. Mother's room was on the first floor of the building, and there was a long line of people standing outside the room, patiently waiting their turn. The line of people went all the way down the stairs and continued out beyond the main entrance of the house and onto the road. Inside Mother's room, some people were sitting in deep meditation, while others simply gazed at Mother in wonderment. The brahmacharins were singing *bhajans*. A professional musician expressed a wish to sing a song about Mother which he himself had set the tune to, *Paravasamannen Hridayam...*

My mind is deeply troubled
by countless distracting thoughts.

O Mother, don't delay anymore!
Take care of this destitute one.

Know that I am helplessly falling
into the depths of the sea.
O Mother
who has been known to us
throughout the ages,
won't You come
and soothe my weeping eyes?

My mind is confused
with all its unfortunate waves.
I am struggling in this ocean of fire
without reaching the shore,
without having beheld
Your Lotus Feet.

A VISION OF MOTHER AS PARASHAKTI

When the song had come to an end, a woman who was in the middle of receiving Mother's *darshan*, suddenly got up and began to dance and sing while she chanted the mantra, "Aum Parashaktyai Namah." The woman raised her arms above her head and joined her palms together. Her eyes were closed and tears were streaming down her cheeks. She looked very blissful. She had the serenity and joy of one who is totally absorbed in meditation.

In her state of bliss the woman exclaimed, "Blessed indeed am I today! By touching Your holy feet I have become blessed and purified. Today, I have seen *Parashakti*.[2] O Mother, please don't leave me!"

Some devotees tried to carry her out of the room. But Mother interrupted and said, "No, no, it's all right! She's in bliss. Don't touch her. Let her dance and sing." Having received Mother's instructions, the devotees gave up the idea of carrying the woman away, and she continued to dance and sing for some time, in the same blissful mood.

Later, the woman talked about her experience:

"As I was waiting in front of Mother, She looked at me and smiled so lovingly. That smile was like a blissful, electric shock to me and all my hairs stood on end. I felt as if I was losing all my body consciousness, and I fell in full prostration in front of Mother. I called out and prayed, 'O Mother, great Enchantress, protect me! O Mother, protect me! O Parvati, Lord Shiva's holy consort, give me refuge!' With infinite love and affection, Mother took hold of me, drew me towards Her and placed my head on Her lap. She then lifted my head from Her lap and applied sandal paste between my eye brows. This divine touch was another supremely blissful experience. My eyes were opened wide. It was like an outer space experience. I was completely im-

---

[2] The Supreme Power, or the Divine Mother

mersed in a divine feeling, its presence so full and tangible, I felt as if I were floating in the air, floating in a feeling of perfect fullness. But what I beheld in front of my eyes was something unbelievable. It was not a dream or an illusion - it was as real and as clear as I am seeing you now."

The woman was very excited. She couldn't speak any more, as her words choked in her throat. Her eyes filled with tears and she seemed ecstatic. The listener who was anxious to hear the last part of her narration said to her, "Kindly tell me about the vision you had. What did you see?"

The lady somehow managed to control her emotions and said, "I saw the beautiful and enchanting form of Devi right in front of my eyes, in all Her splendor and glory, sitting in a lotus posture with all Her weapons. Words cannot begin to describe the wonderful experience I had. My heart was intoxicated with bliss. There was only bliss, bliss, bliss - I was drowning in supreme bliss." Even as she was talking about the experience the lady sounded very blissful.

The four day visit to Calicut was unforgettable. An endless flow of devotees came to seek Mother's blessings. The morning *darshan*, which started at nine-thirty, ended at four or four-thirty each afternoon. Most of the evening programs took place at different public places. People from all walks of life came to meet Mother. There were children, elderly people, *sannyasins*, intellectuals, students, lawyers, doctors, laborers, politicians and journalists. During the morning *darshans*, there was not an inch of space to spare. The way Mother gives *darshan* to the devotees is indescribable. Just as one sees one's own image in a mirror, people see their own true nature, their own Self, in Mother. They feel that the purpose of their lives has been fulfilled. And Mother fulfills their desires; She knows what each one of them wants and it is available in abundance from the inexhaustible source of Her infinite Self.

IS RELIGION RESPONSIBLE FOR THE CONFLICTS OF THE PRESENT DAY?

One journalist who came to see Mother during Her visit to Calicut had the following conversation with Her:
Question: "Amma, religion and spirituality are supposed to guide people on the right path and give them peace of mind. Religious and spiritual people are the ones who have to act as catalysts in bringing harmony and integrity to society and among people, aren't they? But it seems that they are the ones who create a lot of confusion, conflict and a lack of integrity in society. Do you have any explanation for this?"
Mother: "Son, the problem does not lie in religion or spirituality. It lies within the human mind. The essential principles of all religions teach love, peace and harmony. The spiritual masters have never preached

selfishness, nor have they ever encouraged people to fight each other.

"The conflicts and problems of the present day, which exist in the name of religion, are due to the lack of proper understanding about religious principles.

"In this modern age, people live more from their minds than from their hearts. The mind is confusing. It is the dwelling place of selfishness and wickedness. The mind is the seat of all our doubts, and the intellect is the seat of the ego. When you dwell more in the mind and ego, you are concerned only about money, fame and power. You are not concerned about others; you are thinking only about yourself and your status. There are no feelings in your heart. The intellect makes you think, 'I, and I alone.' The mind will keep you busy with all kinds of doubts, suspicions and attachments. Without any faith, love or compassion, hell is created within you.

"The intellectuals interpret; the people believe in those distorted interpretations, and then they fight. This is what is happening in our society. In each religion there are intellectuals and there are minds who listen to them. The intellectuals interpret the teachings of the scriptures and the masters of their religions, and the unsuspecting people fall easy prey to their definitions of the truth, and end up fighting. The intellectuals become leaders and revered advisors. Their followers idealize them and worship them as God. In fact, God has been completely forgotten. The truth and the essential principles of religion have been totally forgotten. The very purpose of religion and religious practices are being ignored.

"Unfortunately most religions are led by intellectuals. The heart alone can guide a person, but the heart has been forgotten. Only a true Master who dwells within the heart can throw light on the path of religion. Such a person alone can unite the people; he alone can make people understand the true import of religion and religious principles.

"No one who has any real understanding of true religion can blame religion and the true religious masters for the present day calamities that are happening in the name of religion. It is the fault of the intellectual interpreters and not their innocent followers. The entire responsibility goes to the pseudo religious teachers, the so-called torch bearers of religion, because they are misguiding people. They want to force their own ideas and evil visions onto others. They are full of their own ideas and interpretations and they want people to listen to them. Their egos crave attention, and because of their greed for recognition, these extremely selfish individuals have made innocent believers pray to them - to their egos. Their innocent followers have full faith in their words, in their false interpretations. Of course, the ego is much more powerful than the mind. The mind is intrinsically weak. The ego has determination, whereas the mind is always doubting, vacillating and unsteady. The intellectual interpreters of almost all religions have the determination to convince people. Their enormous egos and their determination can easily overpower the weak minded followers of any religion. And thus they win their victory over innocent believers, who end up fighting for them.

"Such intellectuals have no faith, or love and compassion. Their mantra is money, power and prestige. Therefore, do not blame religion, spirituality or the true masters for the present day problems. There is nothing wrong with spirituality or religion. The problem lies in the human mind"

The journalist seemed stunned. He was silent for a while before he began to ask another question.

RELIGION AND SPIRITUALITY

Question: "Amma, are spirituality and religion two separate things, or are they one?"

Mother: "Spirituality is the real name of religion. Religion is the outside and spirituality is the inside. Religion can be compared to the outer skin of a fruit and spirituality then, is the real fruit - its essence. Spirituality is the true essence of religion; in fact, they are one and the same. You cannot differentiate between religion and spirituality, but it needs proper discrimination and understanding to penetrate the outer skin and dive deep into the true essence.

"People mistakenly believe that religion and spirituality are two separate entities. But religion and spirituality are as interdependent as body and soul. If viewed and evaluated with the mind and the intellect (ego), you will see it as two. Go a little deeper and you will find that they are one.

"If true religion and religious texts can be compared to the surface of the ocean, spirituality is like the pearls and priceless treasures that lie hidden deep beneath the waters. The real treasure lies deep within.

"The outside of religion, the religious texts and the scriptures, satisfies the intellect, whereas spirituality, which is the inside of religion, gives true happiness and peace of mind because it calms the mind. The search always begins on the outside, but it is bound to culminate on the inside of religion. Through the study of the *Vedas*, the *Upanishads* and other scriptures one may gain a certain amount of intellectual satisfaction. The ego is fed thereby and the mind continues to be turbulent and agitated. But this may cause us to slowly turn from outer religion towards internal religion. When the search on the outside of religion stops, we turn within, and that is spirituality. The outside can never give us complete happiness. One day or another, one has to turn within to the real source. Intellectual happiness can never make us truly happy. You may feel convinced for a moment, but again doubts, questions and reasoning will begin.

"Suppose you get a coconut. But, you have never seen one before. You have heard that it is a very healthy food and that its milk is a wonderful thirst quencher. As you are holding the coconut you see that the outside looks so good and green. You take the outside for the real kernel and you start biting on it. But nothing happens. It's so hard that your gums start bleeding and your teeth ache. You are about to throw the coconut away, when a passerby notices your dilemma. Just when you are about to get rid of it he comes and tells you, 'No, no, don't throw it away! The kernel and the milk are inside. Open it and you will see it.' The man then walks away. Somehow you manage to open the outer shell of the coconut. Now you come upon a cluster of brown fibres and a hard shell. Mistaking the fibre for the kernel you try to chew on it. It is softer than the outside shell, but it tastes funny. The layer underneath is much harder; there is no sense in trying to bite into it. You spit out all the fibre and are about to throw away the coconut in utter desperation. At that moment another person comes up to you. This man has also been watching your struggle. He takes the coconut and opens it for you. You drink the sweet, refreshing water; you eat the kernel and feel fully satisfied. At last your thirst is quenched and your hunger is appeased.

"This is what has happened with spirituality and religion. You mistake the outside for the inside. But the outside is a part of the inside. They are inseparable. The outside is religion and the inside is spirituality. This can also be explained in a different way. Just like the shining outside of a coconut, the human body looks beautiful. People mistake the body for the soul, the Atman, and being strongly attached to the body they focus all their attention on it. One has to go beyond the body to know the Self, one's true essence. But beyond the body exists the far more subtle and complicated mind. Due to their lack of proper understanding, people also believe that the mind is the Atman. To go beyond the mind and its confusing thoughts is much more difficult. Within the mind there exists an even harder shell, made up of the intellect and ego with its sense of 'I' and 'mine.' Only when that is transcended does one reach the kernel, the real Essence. Only a true Master can guide you to that innermost secret of life. Most people are either stuck in the body or in the mind and intellect (ego). Only when one penetrates and goes beyond these three layers can one reach the real abode of happiness, the essence of true religion that is spirituality.

"Just like the outside of a coconut, the outside of religion with all its visual splendor, can be very attractive and alluring. But you won't really get anything out of it, you may even be deluded by it. If you get too attached to the outside, it will only create more pain and more problems.

"Unfortunately, human beings do not have the proper eyes with which to see reality. They are far more attracted to the unreal than to the real, to the outside than to the inside. People are very attached to their own ideas and do not relate to anything else. They live with their own understanding of what religion is, which is very far from true religion.

"Children, here is a story that Amma has heard:

"A group of tourists were travelling through the countryside, when their bus broke down. They were given some food to eat by the natives of the area. But the foreign dishes looked strange to them; they even suspected that the food might be spoiled, and although they were very hungry, they hesitated to eat. Just then, a dog came walking by. The tourists threw a portion of the food to the dog who quickly swallowed it. They studied the dog to see how it would react. But the dog seemed to enjoy the food and suffered no ill effects. The next morning they learned that the dog had died, which meant that the food must have been bad after all. The tourists were shocked. Within a short time many of them were taken seriously ill and suffered from symptoms of food poisoning. A doctor was found. When he was informed about the situation he began to make some inquiries about the whereabouts of the dead dog, intending to take a look at it to verify the cause of death. A person who lived in the area knew what had happened to the dog. He said to the doctor, 'I threw the dog into a ditch, because it had been run over by a car.'

"The reality of religion is something far beyond people's concept about it. The so-called intellectuals of all religions have taught people about a religion that they themselves have created; a religion corresponding to their own ideas, which has little to do with true religion and its essential principles. They fool the people by making them follow only the external aspect of religion, and never the internal. If the internal oneness of religions were to be revealed, their own importance would be greatly diminished and they wouldn't be given any more attention. This is the reason why they highlight only the external differences. Otherwise their egos will starve, which would be unbearable to them. Also, since they, themselves, are stuck in their own intellects, they cannot assimilate the real principles of spirituality; and if they have not imbibed those principles, how can they teach anyone about spirituality?

"Once people come to understand the inner significance of religion, they will leave the false religious leaders. They will no longer seek their guidance, for they will know that only a person who has gone beyond the ego can truly guide them to the real goal of life.

"The essence of all religions of the world is spirituality. A religion without spiritual principles as its base is like an artificial fruit made of wax. Such a religion will be like an artificial limb, lacking any life or vitality. It is like the hollow skin of a fruit, containing no meat.

"Spirituality is the substratum on which all true religions exist. No religion can exist for long if it has no spiritual principles as its foundation. Such a religion would soon die.

"It is like Brahman, the Absolute, and the world of phenomena. The world cannot exist without Brahman, for Brahman is the substratum on which the world exists. But Brahman exists without the world. In a similar manner, religion cannot exist without spirituality. But spirituality exists without religion. It can also be compared to the body and soul (Atman). The soul is needed for the body to exist, but the soul exists without the body. Religion and spirituality are essentially one. If viewed from the right perspective and with the right understanding - they are not two."

CHAPTER SIX

MOTHER STOPS MANIFESTING
KRISHNA BHAVA

O n October 18, 1983, Mother announced that She was going to stop giving Krishna Bhava. This decision created a lot of pain in the hearts of many Krishna devotees. Mother, of course, had Her own reasons for stopping. Mother said, "Amma is in a completely detached mood during Krishna Bhava. In that state Amma doesn't feel any compassion, nor does She feel any lack of compassion. Everything is just a play of consciousness. Amma does not feel touched or affected by anything. But during Devi Bhava it is not like that at all. At that time, She is the Mother who cares deeply for all Her children. Amma feels nothing but love and compassion during Devi Bhava."

Mother Herself has revealed several times that She is both the external and the internal Mother. The external Mother appears as the most compassionate and loving Mother, who cares deeply for Her children. But the inner Mother is beyond all such feelings - like infinite space. Mother says, "If Amma wants, She can remain in the state beyond, completely unaffected and unconcerned, but that wouldn't help much to uplift the suffering and society. This is why Amma chooses the aspect of being a loving and compassionate Mother."

Mother's decision to stop Krishna Bhava soon spread among the residents and devotees. It was shocking news to many of the devotees. Even though they experienced Her divinity both during the divine moods and at all other times, the devotees were very much attached to Amma's Krishna and Devi Bhavas.

In the early days, Mother was very playful and mischievous during Krishna Bhava. She behaved just like Krishna, to the great delight of the devotees.

As far as a *Mahatma* is concerned the world is a delightful play. He is totally detached and unaffected by the diverse and contradictory nature of the world.

Why should there be such a play at all? Since the Lord is the sole ruler of all creation, one may wonder what, is the purpose of this play (*leela*) which He enacts?

Mother once said: "The play of the Supreme Lord has been created only for the sake of enjoying the play. He is the Supreme Ruler and omniscient Reality, but the play can only be a play when it is done without that authority, when the authority is forgotten. The moment you exercise your authority, you step out of the play, and it ceases to be a play.

"Another way to interpret this is that the world seems real only because of our attachment to it. Attachment to the world makes it seem real, while detachment makes it a wondrous play. In the state of detachment there is no feeling of authority. Once you give up your attachment, you realize that everything is only a play and you can then join in.

Mother tells a story to explain this point.

"A little prince was playing with some children on the castle grounds. They were playing hide and seek. The prince was busy searching for his friends and was completely involved in the game, enjoying himself immensely. He couldn't find anyone and he was running here and there, eagerly trying to find the others. A grown up caught hold of the prince and remarked, 'Why are you going through so much trouble to find your friends? They would come to you immediately if you simply were to exercise your royal command and call them?' The prince looked sympathetically at the grown up, as if the poor man were ill, and said, 'But then there would be no game to play and it wouldn't be fun anymore!'

"During Krishna Bhava, Amma is totally detached. In that state of detachment everything is a play. No authority is exercised during Krishna Bhava; whereas, in Devi Bhava, Amma does use Her authority and Her omnipotence to protect Her children."

This playful mood of Amma's during Krishna Bhava created an intense attachment to Amma as Krishna, even though She was surprisingly detached in that state.

One of the most fulfilling moments of Krishna Bhava was when Mother gave the devotees *prasad*, by letting

them drink *panchamritam*[3] directly from the palm of
Her hand, which She brought right up to their lips.
Sometimes, when a devotee opened his or her mouth
to receive the *prasad*, Mother would playfully withdraw
Her hand. She would do this several times to certain
people, especially if they were devotees of Krishna.

Sometimes one could see Mother, as Krishna, playfully tying a devotee's hands together, because he or she
had committed some mistake which Mother knew everything about, without having been told a word about
it. The person had perhaps been fighting with his wife,
or disobeyed some of Mother's words or instructions.
The devotee might have kept quiet about it, but Mother
would catch him when he came for *darshan*.

Once, a young man stopped smoking as a result of
having met Mother. But one day while in the company
of his friends who were smokers, the devotee became
tempted; the pull became so strong that he took just
one puff. But he was so pricked by his conscience that
he refrained from doing it again. During the next Krishna
Bhava when he came up for *darshan*, Mother smiled at
him with a look of mischief in Her eyes. She held Her
middle and index fingers in such a way that it looked
as if She were holding a cigarette, and She brought the
imaginary cigarette right up to Her lips. The young man
was embarrassed and took an oath in front of Mother,

---

[3] A sweet dish, which is offered during worship, made of milk,
bananas, clarified butter, brown sugar, sugar candy and honey.

promising that he would never smoke another cigarette.

On another occasion, Mother covered the mouth of Her paternal grandmother, Acchamma, with a piece of cloth because Acchamma was talking too much. Another time, Mother blind-folded a devotee and ordered him to walk round the temple three times, because he had been watching too many movies. There was an old man who was very innocent, with whom Amma, as Krishna, used to sport mischievously. He was an ardent devotee of Sri Krishna and his faith in Mother was unshakable. Mother always enjoyed playing Her tricks on this childlike old man. He was in his seventies and his eyesight was so poor that without his glasses he couldn't see anything. Whenever he came up for *darshan*, Mother would remove his glasses, and when She did this he used to laugh and laugh until She gave them back to him. Having fixed his glasses on properly, he would move towards Mother to receive Her blessing. But, all of a sudden, Mother would again remove his glasses. Sometimes She did this several times, and the innocent old man just kept on laughing. At some point he would say, "O Krishna, what is this? How can I see You without my glasses?" Then he'd say, "Okay, You can have them. You can take these external glasses and cloud my vision as much as You like, but You can never escape from my mind's eye, or from my heart. You are imprisoned there forever."

Sometimes, during Krishna Bhava, when Mother would feed the old man with *panchamritam*, She continued to feed him without stopping. He would never say that he had had enough; he just kept on gulping it all down. Mother sometimes used to feed him very quickly without even giving him enough time to swallow. When Amma as Krishna saw that he was struggling and getting tired, She laughed sweetly. But it had to stop some time, and when Mother finally stopped feeding him, he protested innocently, "Why did You stop? I like it very much. I want more! Give it all to me!" And sometimes he would say, "Oh Krishna, do You know what? I love the sweetness of Your hand more than the sweetness of any *panchamritam*. That is why I can't say no when You feed me. Sweet are Your hands, oh Lord."

There is a Sanskrit song, *Adharam Madhuram* (*Madhurashthakam*), glorifying Krishna which the old man used to sing when he came up to Mother for *darshan*.

> *Your lips are so sweet*
> *Your face is sweet*
> *Your eyes are sweet*
> *and Your smile is sweet*
> *Your heart is sweet*
> *and sweet is the way that You walk;*
> *O Lord of Mathura*
> *Your whole being is utterly sweet.*

Your words are sweet
and Your stories are sweet
also sweet are the clothes that You wear
Your every movement is sweet;
O Lord of Vrindavan
Your whole being is utterly sweet.

Your flute is so sweet
and Your hands are sweet
and sweet is the dust of Your feet
Your legs are sweet
The way You dance is sweet
Your friendship is sweet;
O Lord of Mathura
Your whole being is utterly sweet.

At the end of each Krishna Bhava, when Mother
was dancing blissfully, the brahmacharins and the devo-
tees used to sing the following *bhajans: Krishna Krishna
Radhe Krishna, Govinda Gopala Venukrishna, Mohana
Krishna Manamohana Krishna, Murare Krishna Mukunda
Krishna, Radhe Govinda Gopi, and Shyama Sundara.*

Mother's divine mood as Krishna was utterly sweet
and enchanting. At the end of Krishna Bhava, She would
come to the entrance of the temple, where She stood for
a long time, looking at the devotees and smiling at them.
And as She stood there, the brahmacharins sang Krishna
bhajans at a high, fervent tempo. Mother then slowly
came out of the temple to the veranda. She raised both
Her arms up high, and with Her hands held in divine
mudras (gestures), She began to dance.

This blissful, ecstatic dance, which was always performed in a gentle, meditative way, invoked a great amount of love and devotion in those who witnessed it. It transported the devotees back to Vrindavan, where Lord Krishna used to sport with the *gopis* and *gopas*. Exactly the same atmosphere and the same vibrations were created by Mother, here, in this small fishing village, for the benefit of the devotees.

The devotees were very attached to Mother's Krishna Bhava, because it was the first Divine Mood that She ever manifested. There were so many memories of Krishna Bhava and the devotees found it difficult to let go. They were in great pain and their agony could clearly be seen reflected in their eyes and movements.

Wherever one went within the Ashram one could hear people talking about their experiences during Krishna Bhava. The innocent old man, who was mentioned earlier, had many wonderful stories to tell. He was constantly recalling how Krishna Bhava began and about the days when Mother used to give Bhava *darshan* on the seashore. He talked about all the great hardships that they had to undergo during that first period.

The devotees were so upset that on Bhava *darshan* days, most of them would burst into tears, first on Krishna's shoulder during Krishna Bhava[4] and then later

---

[4] Mother would always stand during Krishna Bhava, with one foot on a small *peetham* (sacred stool).

on Devi's lap. They prayed to Mother, pleading with Her not to stop the Krishna Bhava. This is why She finally agreed to appear as Krishna once a month. Because of Her infinite compassion towards Her devotees, She could not deny their prayers so easily. But finally, Mother stopped manifesting Krishna Bhava altogether. However, this happened only when Her devotees had gained a much greater spiritual understanding, which allowed them to see that Mother is always the same, whether She is in Krishna Bhava or Devi Bhava. The greater dimension of Her infinite nature was slowly being revealed to Her devotees.

One devotee who was very attached to Mother's Krishna Bhava was telling Br. Balu about one of his experiences. "You know, every evening I place a glass of warm milk in front of a picture of Mother in Krishna Bhava. One day, my wife and I were in such a hurry to leave for the Bhava *darshan* that we didn't have time to cool the milk after it had boiled. It was time for the bus to leave for Vallickavu, so I placed the boiling hot milk in front of the picture in the family shrine room and rushed to the bus stop. The Krishna Bhava had begun when we arrived at the Ashram. My wife and I went up to Mother, who was in the divine mood of Krishna. Like a small, mischievous child, Krishna looked at us and smilingly exclaimed, 'Look! My lips were burnt from drinking the hot milk!' Believe me, a burn mark could actually be seen on Mother's lips!" As the devotee recalled this, tears were streaming down his cheeks. His voice became choked and he couldn't speak anymore due to the uncontrollable emotion that came over him.

A situation similar to that of Krishna leaving Vrindavan was now being created in Mother's Ashram. But, as Mother puts it, "Sometimes this is Krishna and at other times this is Devi. But both Krishna and Devi are always here within this crazy girl." There is a profound teaching hidden in this statement. Since Mother, who in reality is both Krishna and Devi, is living here among us, why should there be any reason to worry? Mother's different aspects, or forms, are not different isolated entities; they are all manifestations of the same Universal Reality. And that one Supreme Reality that is Mother, from whom all forms emerge, is here to protect and to guide us. Therefore there is no point in worrying.

But the despair and the deep sense of loss experienced by the devotees, didn't last for long, because their attachment to Mother was far more deeply rooted than any other consideration.

Over and above all, Mother Herself revealed to everyone that She is one with all these different aspects of the Divine, and that She can manifest any one of them, by Her mere will, at any time She wishes. For instance one day, a few months after Mother had started giving Krishna Bhava only once a month, Mother, Nealu, Balu, Venu and Gayatri were sitting in Nealu's hut. Mother and Nealu were having a conversation, when Nealu suddenly said, "Amma, You are everything to me. You are Krishna, Devi and all the other aspects of the Divine. I know that You are Krishna, and also Radha and Devi. You are verily the embodiment of Brahman. But I still sometimes have an intense thirst to see you in Krishna Bhava."

Mother gave Nealu a mischievous smile and asked, "Nealumon (Nealu my son), do you really want to see Mother in Krishna Bhava?"

"Yes, very much!" replied Nealu. Without another word, Mother took hold of Nealu's cotton shawl and tied it around Her head. Turning around to Nealu, She said, "Look!" Those present were amazed to see Mother sitting there, looking exactly as She would during Krishna Bhava. The way She held Her hands in sacred *mudras* and all Her facial expressions - the sparkling eyes and the way She smiled[5] - all were exactly the same.

The brahmacharins and Gayatri spontaneously prostrated before Her. But the divine revelation lasted for only a few seconds, and Mother resumed her conversation with Nealu.

Once, Br. Pai wanted a certain image of Mother that he had a special love for. He had a few photographs of Mother, including ones of Her as Devi and Krishna, and of course he liked them all, but this spe-

---

[5] During Krishna Bhava, Mother used to smile with a peculiar downward bent of Her lips, which was very attractive.

cial image, which had yet to be photographed, was a picture of Mother sitting in a certain posture. It was the image of Her on which he meditated. He had an intense wish to have a photo of Mother, sitting in exactly that posture on the Devi Bhava *peetham*, but in Her ordinary white clothes and with Her hair tied up, without the crown. He also wanted Mother to display the classical *abhaya mudra* of protection and blessing.[6] But how could he ask Mother to sit in a particular pose in order to take a snap shot? He did not open his heart to anyone about this.

One day, Pai couldn't bear it anymore. He felt very sad about this matter and wept for a long time. Suddenly Mother came walking towards him. She smiled at him and said, "Son, Amma knows your desire. Don't worry, Amma will fulfill it." She told Pai to follow Her and went into the temple. Mother seated Herself on the Devi Bhava *peetham* exactly in the same posture that Pai had visualized. But the moment Mother sat down on the *peetham*, Her mood changed. She became exactly like Devi, expressing all the divine signs that She would normally manifest during Devi Bhava. Br. Srikumar took the photograph and Pai's long cherished dream was fulfilled. The most important point to remember here is Mother's power to manifest both

---

[6] In this *mudra* both palms are open, facing outward with the fingers held together. The right hand is held at the shoulder and the left hand is pointing downward towards the hip.

Krishna and Devi, or any divine mood, at any time She wills. It is not something that is limited to a certain time or place. Whenever and wherever She chooses to be in that mood, that is the right time and place for it.

In the early days, the few brahmacharins who were staying at the Ashram used to chant the *Sri Lalita Sahasranama,* the thousand names of Devi, with Mother seated on a special *peetham* for that purpose. But sometimes Mother preferred to sit on the Devi Bhava *peetham*. There were many occasions when Mother fulfilled the brahmacharins' wishes and even wore the Devi Bhava costume, including the crown, during this special chanting of the thousand names. The brahmacharins would sit in a semicircle in front of Mother and perform the worship, which took one and a half to two hours to complete. Throughout this time Mother would be deeply absorbed in *samadhi*. Her appearance was then exactly the same as in Devi Bhava. There were occasions when Mother remained in *samadhi* even after the chanting and worship were over.

There were countless occasions when Mother clearly revealed Her oneness with the Divine, or when She spoke openly about it. These revelations, coupled with some profound experiences which gave the brahmacharins and devotees a deeper insight into Mother's real nature, helped them to gain more spiritual maturity and understanding.

The last regular Krishna Bhava *darshan* was an unforgettable night. The devotees, one after the other, burst into tears on Krishna's shoulder. Only Krishna *bhajans* were sung that night, and finally when the brahmacharins ran out of Krishna *bhajans*, they chose songs about Devi, songs that were poignant with longing, and converted them into Krishna *bhajans*. Br. Venu was in tears throughout the entire Krishna Bhava. Finding himself unable to sing, he got up and went inside the temple. Mother let him sit close by Her side.

One of the songs they chose to sing that night will give the reader an idea about the mental agony that the devotees were going through. It was *Povukayayo Kanna...*

> *O Kanna, are You leaving?*
> *I have been abandoned*
> *by everyone in this world*
> *Are You also forsaking me?*

> *O Kanna*
> *I want to keep You*
> *as a blue jewel*
> *in the chamber of my heart*
> *and worship You there*
> *each day.*

> *O Kanna*
> *let me gather the pearls of Love*
> *from the depths of the blue ocean*
> *that is Your form.*

> *And when You come to me*
> *in the guise of a blissful bird*
> *the mournful bird of my life*
> *will long to merge with You*
> *O Kanna.*

The regular manifestation of Mother's Krishna Bhava ended that night. However, as has already been mentioned, for the sake of Her devotees, Mother continued to appear as Krishna once a month, until November 1985 when the last Krishna Bhava took place.

Let us close this chapter by recalling a few of Mother's words:

"Devotees call this 'Krishna,' 'Devi,' 'Shiva,' 'Mother,' or 'Guru,' according to their faith. Amma is none of these, and at the same time She is everything. But She is also beyond. The entire universe exists as a small bubble within Her."

CHAPTER SEVEN

devotee, who lived four kilometers south of the Ashram, had invited Mother to his home, and Mother had promised him that She would come.

This evening, at about ten o'clock, after the evening *bhajans*, Mother, along with a few brahmacharins (Balu, Srikumar, Pai, Venu and Rao), Damayanti-amma, Harshan, Satheesh and two other ladies from the neighborhood, set out walking along the ocean, towards the devotee's house. It was a beautiful night. The full moon shone in the sky, and in the moonlight the Arabian Sea glittered, its waves reverberating with the sacred sound, "Aum". Now and then the clouds would cover the moon for a few seconds and it would suddenly become dark. But soon again, the face of the earth would be lit up by the moon's milky light.

The party moved slowly southwards with the sea to their right. At the beginning of the journey no one spoke as they walked. When they had gone about half a kilometer, Mother suddenly went up to the edge of the water where the waves washed the shore. She stood there gazing towards the western horizon, while the waves washed Her sacred feet, over and over again, as

if they wanted to do it as many times as they could
before She continued on Her way.

AS VAST AND DEEP AS THE OCEAN

As Mother was standing there, a few words slipped
from Her lips. She said, "The ocean is vast and expan-
sive, but it is also deep. You can see and experience the
vastness to some extent, whereas its depth is invisible
and beyond your normal vision. To know it you have
to dive in. But to take that deep plunge you need self-
surrender, courage and an adventurous mind."

Mother was silent after this, and they continued walking towards the South. Along the way one of the brahmacharins asked Mother a question. "Amma," he said,
"what did You mean by what You said when You were
standing at the edge of the water?"

Mother answered and said, "Children, you can experience a *Mahatma's* love, compassion, self-sacrifice and
other godly qualities. You can experience these qualities on a large scale in the presence of a Great Soul.
It can be compared to seeing the vastness of the ocean.
You can see the vastness to a certain extent, but you
cannot see all of it. You may get a glimpse of it, an
infinitesimal portion of it, but it is nothing. Viewing
the ocean from the shore is nothing. But although you
are actually seeing just a tiny bit of it, it allows you to
grasp the fact that the ocean is immeasurably vast.

"The ocean is deep and vast. The depth is within and the vastness without. The love and compassion of a *Mahatma* that we experience can be compared to the vastness of the ocean. The *Mahatma's* love and compassion is an external manifestation which gives us a tangible experience of that which lies within. But, we do not know how to be completely open like children, and because of this, the experience of infinite love and compassion showered upon us by a *Mahatma* is only partially felt by us. We are only able to experience a fraction of his or her divine qualities. But that which lies within, that immeasurable depth, is like the depth of the ocean. It is not visible to us. To experience that depth one has to penetrate the surface and go beyond. One should see beyond the love which is manifested outwardly.

BOW DOWN AND KNOW THE DEPTH

"The outer form (of a *Mahatma*) is certainly beautiful and spectacular, and outer association is relatively easy, whereas inner contact is not that easy. It can be compared to swimming and diving. Swimming on the surface of the ocean is a pleasant and joyful experience. But diving can be a far greater experience. It is an adventure. As you dive in, you are entering an entirely different world of experience. You are going to explore the unknown and mysterious realms of the ocean. But it needs a greater effort than just swimming on the surface. You have to hold your breath and bow down before the ocean as you go beneath the waters. The swimmer thus surrenders to the ocean. And when you surrender, the ocean reveals its hidden treasures to you. Until now you have only seen the beautiful surface; you never thought that there could be far more beautiful areas yet to be explored. As you dive deeper and deeper, you find that you want to see more and more, you want to experience more of its depths. You will feel an unquenchable thirst for knowledge. And so, you dive deeper and deeper until you reach the very ground of the ocean.

"In a similar manner, a *Mahatma's* external expressions of love and compassion are extraordinarily beautiful. It is incomparable. There is nothing like it on the face of the earth. But even more so, the beauty of his inner Self is utterly beyond words. In order to experience that hidden beauty, the beauty of unfathomable depths, one has to go beyond the body of the *Mahatma*. One has to go beyond the surface expressions of love and compassion. To reach that which is inexpressible, one has to go beyond all forms of expression. To be able to penetrate the surface and go beyond the external form of the *Mahatma*, one needs to bow down and surrender to him with complete humility. It is like taking a deep plunge into the ocean. Once you completely surrender, the *Mahatma* will reveal his inner nature to you.

"The love of a *Mahatma* is beyond words. The love that you see and experience outwardly is of course deep and intense, but that depth and intensity is only an infinitesimal fraction of what he or she really is. And that is infinite. When something is infinite, you can speak or write about it endlessly without ever coming to a satisfactory explanation, because it has no limit. It is vaster than the universe.

"Being an embodiment of love and compassion, the *Mahatma* is as patient as the earth. But it can also be said that the anger of a *Mahatma* has exactly the same depth as the love, compassion and patience that he or she expresses."

Mother stopped talking. The time was almost eleven p.m. Some fishermen were still wandering on the seashore, others were lying here and there, sleeping on the sand. In the moonlight one could see a group of fishermen sitting on the beach, talking and gossiping. During the moments when the clouds covered the moon, it was possible to discern only the burning ends of their beedies.[7] Some of those who were roaming about came nearer to take a closer look at the small group of people walking along the ocean at this late hour. When they recognized familiar faces, they left without saying anything.

One person who came to look at them happened to be a devotee. When he discovered that it was Mother and the

---

[7] Inexpensive Indian cigarettes rolled in a leaf, commonly used by the poor.

brahmacharins, he became very excited. "Oh! Is it you, Ammachi?" He exclaimed. "Where are you going at this time of the night?" The man called out to his wife and children, "Come here! Come and see who it is!" His wife and their three daughters appeared in no time. They were all very excited to see Mother and the others. They invited Mother to their hut. Politely and lovingly Mother declined the invitation, saying, "Children, Amma is already late. We were walking too slowly since we were talking about spiritual matters, and in between, we spent some time just standing on the beach. Amma is sorry. She will come another time." The man gave his wife a mild scolding for inviting Mother in such an odd manner. He said, "What is this? Is this the way to invite Ammachi to our home? Even though Ammachi is very unassuming in Her manners, we should invite Her in the traditional way, and not as if we were inviting a friend or a neighbor."

The woman was embarrassed and said in a defensive tone, "I am uneducated and illiterate. I don't know any traditions. Ammachi knows this and She will surely forgive me if I have committed a mistake."

Mother turned to the husband and said, "Son, it's okay. Where there is true love, there is no need of *acharas* (customary observances). Her invitation was innocent. There is no greater *achara* than love."

Mother turned to the woman and gave her a hug, saying, "Daughter, don't worry. Take it easy. Amma

will visit your home when She has time. But today,
Amma won't be able to come."

Mother did not forget to also express Her love towards their daughters. She was about to leave when the
man called out, "Ammachi, may I come with you?"

Mother said to him, "Yes, son, of course you may come."
Without even changing into a clean dhoti, he began to
follow Mother.

Mother and the group continued on their way, accompanied by the surging drone of the ocean and a cool
wind blowing from the West. Mother was gazing at the
ocean as She walked. The sea was glowing dark and
blue in the moonlight.

LIKE THE PRALAYAGNI
(THE FIRE OF DISSOLUTION)

As they were walking, another question was asked:
"Amma, you stated that the *Mahatma's* anger has the
same depth as his patience, and his love and compassion. What do you mean by that?"

Mother continued to gaze towards the ocean for
some time before She answered.

"Children, *Pralayagni*, the fire of dissolution - that
is what the anger of a *Mahatma* is like. It is as fierce as
the final dissolution. A *Mahatma* is one with infinity, so
even his anger is of an infinite dimension. You cannot
imagine its intensity. It has the power to destroy the

whole world. It is like dropping countless nuclear bombs simultaneously. Its flames can consume the entire world.

"When the Mother of the Universe, the embodiment of love and compassion, who loves and cares for the entire creation, got angry, She became Kali, and Her anger was as fierce as *Pralayagni*, the fire of dissolution. The entire universe would have been burned into a handful of ashes, if the celestial beings had not intervened.

"When the Universal Mother becomes angry, it is a dazzling sight - like billions of suns ablaze at the same time. Who could bear such a thing? Only one who is egoless and who has completely surrendered can bear it. The infinite power of Kali's anger can only be born by one who has gone beyond body-consciousness. In other words, only consciousness in its pure, motionless form can bear it. The anger of the Universal Mother is a violent tempest of consciousness, so to speak. It can only be counterbalanced by an energy that is perfectly motionless; and that is Shiva lying prostrate, while Kali dances out all Her fury on top of Him.

"Kali's rage is *rajas* in its extreme state. It is the explosion of the cosmic energy with all its power and glory. It is like the explosion of a hundred thousand atom bombs. But even this analogy is insufficient. The explosion of this energy can only be counter balanced by pure *sattvic* energy, and that is Shiva.

"Recall how fierce Sri Rama became when the ocean

would not yield to His prayers. In order to please the ocean, so that He could build a bridge across it, Sri Rama sat down on the seashore and performed severe austerities continuously for three days. He wanted to cross the ocean and reach Lanka, the abode of Ravana who had kidnapped Sita, Rama's holy consort. His intention was to rescue Sita with the help of the monkey army, led by Hanuman and Sugreeva. But the ocean would not yield. It continued raising gigantic waves and became more turbulent than ever.

"Sri Rama was the Supreme Lord Himself, the Master of all creation. He did not have to be humble towards any one of His creatures, and there was no need for Him to be so humble towards the ocean. But He acted with humility because He wanted to set an example. However, the great epic, the *Ramayana*, says that when He did this the ocean became proud, and this made Sri Rama terribly angry, that is, he commanded anger to come. Taking His great bow and stringing an arrow to it, the Lord in His fierce form stood up and said, 'I have tried to be humble and patient, obeying the set laws of Nature. But do not consider it to be a weakness on my part. With this single arrow I can dry up your entire waters and destroy every living creature within you. Should I do this, or are you going to yield?' And the ocean yielded by subsiding its waves.

"Sri Rama was the personification of supreme patience and forgiveness. He had even forgiven Kaikeyi,

His stepmother, who had been extremely cruel towards Him. But when He now became angry, His anger was as deep as His patience. The *Ramayana* says that when Rama stood with the bow and arrow in His hands, ready to charge at the ocean, He looked like the God of Death, the fire of final dissolution."

THE HIGHEST PEAK OF HUMAN EXISTENCE

Mother continued, "Self-Realization is the highest peak of human existence. It is the final point of concentration (one-pointedness). There is no point beyond that. The depth and energy of such concentration is indescribably piercing. The Self-Realized soul has used that power of concentration to penetrate into the deepest mystery of the universe, the mystery of Brahman. In that supreme state of Self-Realization he has become an adept in concentration, and with his absolute one-pointedness he can concentrate and direct his energies wherever and whenever he wishes. A true Master will never use his power for any destructive purpose. He always uses it for the good of the world and for the uplift of society. But remember that he can also use it to teach the entire human race a lesson. A Self-Realized Master is one with the Cosmic Energy, and that energy is infinite. He can release it or hold it or do whatever he wishes with it. He can choose to release either positive or negative energy. But even if he should release it in a seemingly negative way, it is only for the good of the world; it is done only for the sake of teaching someone a lesson.

"So, whether that energy is released positively or negatively, it will have its intended effect. Either way, its power will be infinite, beyond words. Just as the divine love and compassion of a *Mahatma* is beyond words, his anger is also beyond words. There is no way to measure the depths of a *Mahatma*."

Mother's words remind one of a song, *Ananta Srishti Vahini*, written by one of Her devotees about Mother's infinite moods.

> *Salutations to You*
> *O Great Divine Goddess*
> *the Support of all creation*
> *who has infinite states of Being*
> *and is eternally dancing*
> *the Supreme Dance.*
>
> *Salutations to You*
> *O Ever-Effulgent One*
> *Mother of Immortal Bliss*
> *who unceasingly breaks the silence*
> *of the dead of night.*
>
> *Prostrations to You,*
> *O Bhadrakali,*
> *the fierce form of Devi,*
> *the cause of all that is auspicious,*

who permeates all consciousness,
who is full of compassion.
You are the One who dissolves
the individual.
Prostrations to You
whose form is like a triangle[8]
who had three eyes,
who carries the trident
and wears a garland of skulls.
O Bhairavi,
You bestow good fortune
and live in the cremation grounds.

Prostrations to You
O Chandika
ever-increasing
fierce and effulgent
infinitely strong
who swings Her sword,
making the sound "Jhana, Jhana."

Prostrations to You
O Goddess Chandika
who is full of radiance.
You are Shankari
and Your Power is infinite.
You are the giver of all yogas
and of immortality.

---

[8] Referring to the triangles in the Sri Chakra *yantra*.

Mother and the group reached the house at eleven-fifteen. The whole family was eagerly awaiting Mother's arrival, and they were overjoyed when She arrived. The head of the family, along with his wife, received Mother with the traditional *pada puja* (washing of the sacred feet) and *arati* (the offering of light), after which they all prostrated at Mother's feet. Mother expressed Her love and affection to everyone in the family in Her usual manner, and there was real joy among them. The youngest child, a boy who was barely four years old, was dancing gleefully saying loudly, "Amma has come! Oh, Amma has come to our house!" Mother called the boy to come to Her and She showered him with kisses. Having received Her kisses he looked even more joyful.

The worship started at midnight and was completed by two in the morning. After the *puja*, Mother went outside and sat in the backyard looking out across the ocean. There was deep silence everywhere except for the sound of the ocean, chanting its eternal hymn. Mother, in Her white sari, sat swaying gently back and forth in the moonlight.

As Mother was sitting there, the whole family and the group from the Ashram came out and sat at a slight distance, from where they could see Mother. No one wanted to sit very close to Her, for they all knew that Mother was revelling in Her own world of Aloneness.

THE COMPASSIONATE MOTHER

The return journey started at two-thirty in the morning. There wasn't much talk during the walk back, but Mother sang a few *bhajans*.

When they reached the home of the devotee who had accompanied them from the beach, he stepped forward to take leave of Mother. To his great surprise Mother turned towards his house and said, "Amma is coming with you." The man was dumbfounded for a second and stood frozen like a statue. He almost shouted in excitement as he said, "What! Are You coming to my house!" Soon he could be seen running at full speed towards his house. He pounded on the door, calling out his wife's and children's names. He was all in a flurry and did not know what to do. He ran hither and thither in front of his home calling his wife and children, again and again. Within a few seconds the whole family were wide awake. They were completely startled. They could not understand why he was making so much noise at this odd hour of the night. The wife shot several questions at her husband, all in one breath. "What has happened to you! Why are you shouting like this? Didn't you go with Ammachi?" A neighbor had also been awakened by all the commotion. He called out from the veranda of his house, "My friends, what is going on? Do you want me to come over?"

By this time Mother had reached the front yard.

The devotee's wife stood staring with her mouth wide open when she noticed Mother standing, smiling in front of her. The children were also stunned. At first, the woman could not speak. A moment later she burst into tears and fell on Mother's shoulder. The man was already lying prostrate at Her feet, weeping like a child. Mother raised the man and lay his head on Her other shoulder. His wife managed to say through her tears, "Am I dreaming, Ammachi? O God, what *leela* (play) is this! You should have told me that You were going to visit us on your way back. I would have prepared everything and waited for You! Now, there is nothing in the house. The oil lamp hasn't even been lit! O Amma, why are You playing this *leela* with us?"

The woman cried uncontrollably. Mother tried to console her saying, "Daughter, Amma is not a guest. She is your Mother. There is no need of any elaborate preparations to receive Her. Your love for Her is more than enough, there is nothing to worry about. Whatever you offer with your own hands is like ambrosia to Amma. Don't cry!" But the innocent woman couldn't stop crying. Finally, Mother took the initiative and walked into the house with Her arms around the woman.

It was a hut with two small rooms and a tiny kitchen. Mother went straight into the kitchen followed by the woman, her husband and their three daughters, while the others waited outside. Mother searched through the kitchen; She looked inside the pots and pans, but everything was empty. And as Mother was searching, the woman kept saying, "What a pity! There is nothing to eat in the house!" At last Mother found a tapioca root lying in a corner. "Ah, this will be more than enough!" She said and picked it up. Mother bit into the root as She walked out of the kitchen.

It so happened that Harshan had been carrying a bag with fried edibles from the other house which they had visited. Mother took some of that food and began to feed the family with Her own hands. Their joy and gratitude knew no bounds. With tears in her eyes, the woman began to sing a few lines from a *bhajan*, *Ammayalle Entammayalle*, and soon the whole family joined in.

Aren't You my Mother?
O, aren't You my dear Mother
who wipes away my tears?

O Mother of the fourteen worlds
the Creatrix of the world
I have been calling You endlessly!
O Shakti!
Won't You come?

O You, who loves to give us
all that we desire
who contains within Yourself
creation, preservation and destruction,
I have been calling You endlessly!

O Father and Mother,
the five different elements
and all the Earth,
I have been calling You endlessly!

The Vedas and the scriptures
true Knowledge and Vedanta
the beginning, the middle and the end
all exist within You.
I have been calling You endlessly!

After spending a few more minutes with the family, Mother returned to the Ashram.

CHAPTER EIGHT

LEARN TO CONQUER BOREDOM

A visiting devotee, known for his questioning nature, asked Mother, "Amma, the majority of people usually get bored when they do the same work, the same thing, day in and day out. That is why people want to change their lives; they want to try a new job, buy different things, etc. But Amma, You are doing the same thing every single day, receiving people and giving them *darshan*. Don't You ever feel bored with the same routine, over and over again?"

Mother: "Son, boredom happens only to human beings, not to God. God never gets bored. A *Mahatma* is God Himself, in a human form, who is ever established in the Absolute Brahman. He constantly experiences a sense of wonder and freshness in his outlook and in all his actions. He is the Immanent Consciousness which shines in and through everything. Therefore he cannot be bored.

"Boredom and dryness come only when you have a feeling of duality, the attitude of 'I' and 'you,' when you believe that you are a separate entity. If you are everything, how can you be bored? Oneness with the entire universe eliminates any such feelings. When you are content within your own Self, boredom automatically disappears.

"A *Mahatma* is like a lake filled with pure, crystal clear water, with a bottom made of solid rock, from which a never ending spring gushes forth. The substratum is firm and immovable, and at the same time it is constantly producing pure, clean water. The spring of water is unending, it will never dry up. It is eternally full, and it allows everyone to drink from it.

"A *Mahatma* knows that he is the changeless and indestructible Atman, or Brahman, the Substratum of the entire universe, and this knowledge makes him firm and immovable within. He is also a never-ending source of love and compassion.

"When your existence is rooted in pure love, how can you ever be bored? Boredom comes only when you do not love. There is no sense of separation in true love. Love just flows. Whoever is willing to take the plunge and dive in, will be accepted as they are. There are no terms or conditions. If you are willing to take the dip you will be accepted. If you are not willing, what can it do? The stream remains where it is. It never says no. It is constantly saying yes, yes, yes...

SAY 'YES' TO LIFE

"To accept is to say yes to everything. Everything may go wrong in your life, but still, you find yourself saying, 'Yes, I accept.' The river says yes to everyone. All of Nature say yes, except human beings. A human being can say both yes and no. Sometimes he says yes, but mostly he says no. He doesn't see life as a gift; he sees it as a right, and he also considers happiness to be a right. When you see life, and all that life brings you, as a precious gift, you will be able to say yes to everything. If, on the other hand, you insist on seeing it as a right, then you cannot say yes - you can only say no. That is where everything goes wrong. If you always say no to life, to all the experiences that life brings you, you will be miserable and you will get bored. But if you learn to always say yes, if you can see life and each experience as a gift, and not as a right, you will never be conquered by boredom.

"When you are full of love and compassion, you cannot say no to anything, you can only say yes. Amma can only say yes. She never says no, and therefore, She doesn't get bored. 'Yes' is acceptance. Only when there is acceptance is there no boredom.

"The word 'no' exists only where duality exists. When you say no to life you feel unhappy and discontented. You will protest about everything and you cannot be happy with yourself. You always feel insignificant and unsatisfied. Why is this? Because you are always wanting. You want money, fame, a new house, a new car, the list goes on and on. Thus you become unhappy, you get bored and life becomes dry. You become a constant complainer who isn't satisfied with anything. Why? Because you insist on constantly saying no. Due to your lack of acceptance, you are unable to say yes to whatever life provides you with.

"People are always chasing after things. That is why, in spite of all their education and intellectual knowledge, people are still unhappy and they still feel inadequate. Even the wealthiest people are unhappy. They still get easily bored and are plagued by numerous desires, because they are dissatisfied and feel that they have yet to become complete.

"Life is a precious gift. But we don't use our discrimination to choose what is right. We choose the wrong things and then we end up feeling unhappy. So the problem lies within ourselves. It is our wrong attitude that brings us discontentment and boredom. We give too much importance to that which is only secondary, while the most important, primary things are completely ignored."

Mother then proceeded to tell a story to clarify this point.

"A person was suffering from two different ailments. His eyes were troubling him and he also had digestive problems. He went to a doctor, who gave him some eye drops and some medicine for his stomach. He was to put a few drops of the eye medicine in his eyes and to take several spoons of the stomach medicine for his indigestion. But unfortunately, in his excitement the patient confused the doctor's instructions. He went home and drank a dose of the eye drops and poured stomach medicine into his eyes, with the result that both his problems became more aggravated.

"Likewise, there is great confusion with regard to our own lives. We need to give far more importance to the soul, to the realization of the Self, so that we can lead truly contented, blissful lives. And we ought to give far less importance to the body. But we are doing it the other way around; we are mixing up the two containers, taking the wrong medicine for the wrong ailment. All the energy, care and attention that we are meant to direct towards the soul, are being given to the body instead, as we concentrate on making the body as beautiful and comfortable as possible. But the soul is barely given a drop of our attention and is left to its own fate. In our state of confusion we have lost our sense of perspective, with the result that we think and act in a negative way, and we feel bored and very discontented.

"When you are established in the Self you are in an incessantly giving mood. You cannot feel bored when you constantly want to give, when you do not want anything from anyone. Amma just wants to give. She doesn't need anything from anyone, and She doesn't expect anything. Amma simply accepts everything that happens in her life. It is because of this that Amma never gets bored.

"Only when the feeling of being separate disappears can you become a person who gives incessantly.

All sense of duality should go, which means that the mind should go. Only then can you become a true giver who doesn't need to take or receive anything. Boredom comes only from being selfish and self-centered. When you are centered in the Atman, when your center shifts from the self to the Self, and you have no other center, that is when you are completely free from getting bored.

"Radha's love for Sri Krishna never died, and Mira's love for her beloved Giridhar never died either. Neither one of them ever expected anything in return for their love. They were both great givers, and they were never bored - only blissful and content. Whatever they received, whether good or bad, was appreciated and accepted wholeheartedly. This is why they are still living in the hearts of people. And they became immortal because they gave up everything. You only truly begin to live when you die to your ego - to your mind. Radha and Mira were dead to their egos. Mira said, 'O, my Giridhar, it is okay if you do not love me. But my Lord, don't ever take away my right to love You.' This was her attitude. Radha and Mira were completely selfless. Their love was pure, untainted by the ego and selfish thoughts.

"When you live as an ego, obeying your mind, acting according to its whims and fancies, you are not yourself - you are the mind. It is a form of insanity. It is as if you were dead, because you are living as a mere body and mind, without being aware of your real existence as the Self. If you believe that you are the body, you are leading a life of illusion. Isn't it madness to consider the unreal to be real, to superimpose upon reality that which does not belong to it? As long as you live in the mind, you will continue to be bored.

"The burden and constant noise of your mind is a heavy load to carry. It has become an enormous load, enough to overwhelm you. The pitiful thing about this is that you who are carrying this load are not aware of its terrible weight.

"Thinking that your boredom is caused by external situations and by other people, you run from one place to another, you try out as many things as possible, until you finally collapse. Don't you want to unload the burden of your mind, to feel free and at peace? 'Yes, I would like to,' is the answer of most people. But they do not want to release their grip on that to which they are holding. They think that if they let go, they will become vulnerable and insecure.

"Even a small child has this feeling. If a child is not with its mother or father, it will feel very insecure. Children always walk around holding onto one end of their mother's sari or their father's shirt. This makes them feel secure and protected. But, it won't last for long, because the source of security will shift. As the child grows, the feeling of insecurity will also grow, and he discovers that being with his parents is not real security. He will even begin to feel that his parents are an obstacle to his freedom. He will soon begin to feel that there is something or somebody else that can provide him with more contentment than his parents or his home or the city where he lives. Discontentment and boredom go hand in hand. You become bored with your parents, so you want to be away from them. You feel bored in your home and in your city, so you want to live somewhere else. You are bored with your old car, so you want a new one, you are bored with your old girlfriend, so you want a different one. In your search for security and contentment, you constantly embrace insecurity. But you never find that contentment. You just continue to come face to face with your insecurity and discontentment.

"It is your mind that is insecure. It is your mind that creates your boredom and your fears, and is the cause of all your problems. Get rid of the mind rather than trying to replace one object or place with another. Rid yourself of the mind, and you will become a new person with a fresh, ever new outlook on life. As long as you carry the mind with you, you will remain the same old person endowed with the same fears, insecurity, boredom and discontentment.

"Real security in life can be found only in the Self (Atman), or God. And the only way to get rid of your boredom is to surrender to your own Self, to God, or to a perfect Master. Be a witness to everything that happens in life. You are the eternal *Purusha*. You are *Purnam* (Perfection). You are the Whole, and not a limited individual. Remove all your feelings of sorrow, boredom, and discontentment. Be blissful and content."

When the conversation ended, no one felt like saying anything. The explanation which Mother had just given was so beautiful and revealing, that if anyone had earlier wanted to ask a question, it was now forgotten. Mother was sitting with Her eyes closed. Everyone spontaneously did the same, and sitting with closed eyes, in a contemplative mood, they drank in and relished the spiritual feeling that was tangibly present in the atmosphere.

Later, when everyone began to come out of their meditative mood, Mother asked the brahmacharins to sing a song, *Sukhamenni Tirayunna*.

You, who are searching
for happiness everywhere,
how will you find it
without shedding your vanity?
Until the compassionate One,
the Mother of the Universe,
shines within your heart
How can you be happy?

The mind
in which devotion towards Shakti,
the Supreme Power,
is not alive
is like a flower without fragrance.

Such a mind will be forced
to toss about in misery
like a leaf
tossed by the waves
of the restless ocean.

Do not get caught in the talons
of the vulture known as fate
Worship the Self in seclusion
Stop expecting the fruits
of your actions
Worship the form of the Universal Self
in the blossom of your heart.

CHAPTER NINE

THE INCOMPREHENSIBLE MOTHER

*E*ven people who are very close to Mother have always felt that She is incomprehensible. After several years of close association with Mother, the author personally feels that there is something impenetrable about Mother, that She is somebody who is far beyond his understanding.

The first group of brahmacharins who came to Mother have always wondered, "How is it possible to understand Mother? How are we to know Her wishes so that we can act and serve Her accordingly?" Sometimes they have run into trouble because of their difficulties in understanding Mother.

They have on countless occasions experienced Mother's impregnable nature. It is easy to understand the nature of a person, if we move in close proximity with him or her for some time, a few weeks or maybe even months. But after nearly two decades Mother remains a completely unknown personality to the first brahmacharins and to everyone who has come close to Her. Bri. Gayatri, who today is known as Swamini Amritaprana, and who has been serving Mother for two decades, once stated about Mother, "What phenomenon is this? Even infinity can be understood, but not Mother!"

Once, Br. Balu was with Mother in Her room. Bri. Gayatri was also present. Mother was being very loving and affectionate towards Balu. She talked to him for a long time, put all his doubts at rest and answered all his questions. She even fed him with Her own hands. He was feeling filled with Mother's love, and with joy and bliss. But all of a sudden, Mother turned around and asked him to get out of the room. No trace of love could be seen on Her face. She was completely detached. Balu was shocked to see this sudden change in Mother, and felt utterly confused. At first he thought that Mother was playing a game with him, but he soon realized that She was being serious. He wanted to ask why, because he didn't understand what was happening. He wanted to ask but he couldn't, because Mother's words and the forbidding look on Her face were of such depth and power that he didn't dare. This sudden change in Mother's mood was like throwing a big rock in the still, calm waters of a lake; it was as if a beautiful castle was crumbling to pieces at the very moment when its beauty was being admired and appreciated.

Balu remained silent and stood like a statue in the room. He could barely move when he heard Mother's voice repeat, "Get out! I want to be alone! Why should it take you so long to leave?" With a heavy, broken heart Balu slowly walked out of the room, and just as he crossed the threshold, Mother shut the door with a bang. The sound of the door was like an unbearably hard blow which had been aimed at Balu's heart.

Even though he had left Mother's room, Balu couldn't bring himself to move away from the door. His attachment to Mother was so intense that he sat down in front of the closed door to Her room and cried like an abandoned child.

Balu thought, "This must be a real test of my faith and patience. Of course, one gets a little puffed up when Mother allows one to be close to Her for some time. The ego thinks, 'I must be very special, otherwise, why would Mother let me be this close to Her for such a long time?' It is then that Mother's thunderbolt falls upon you. The problem is that the mind never thinks, 'How fortunate and blessed I am to spend so much time in Mother's presence.' The mind and ego can only think negatively in terms of selfishness and pride. When Mother's unexpected attack comes, one's pride is shattered. If there is no pride, if there is only a good and positive feeling of how blessed I am and how gracious Mother is, then there can be no question of feeling sad and upset. Pain and sadness come when the role of the ego is questioned. If I don't feel proud and think that I am special, because I spend so much time with Mother, and that I have a right to be in Mother's presence, then there cannot be any sadness. How can I feel sad or upset when there is only humility?"

A few minutes later he heard somebody open the door. He raised his head and was surprised to see Mother standing there with a big smile on Her face. Her mood was the same as it had been before She had told Balu to get out. As if nothing had happened She now said to him, "Come in, son. But what happened to you! Why are you crying?" Balu could hardly believe it. It took a few moments for him to comprehend what was happening. As he stood there, wondering about the strangeness of it all, Balu once again heard Mother's voice, "Son, come in. What happened? Why are you crying?" Those words were like a burst of rain to the chataka bird of Balu's heart.[9] All the pain of his heart melted away, like ice in the scorching heat of the sun. He was so overwhelmed by Mother's compassion that he burst into tears all over again. But he couldn't help wondering to himself about the apparent contradiction in Mother's nature. At first She had been so loving and affectionate, and then suddenly, for no apparent reason, She had become completely detached. What had happened? He simply couldn't understand. A few minutes later he asked, "Mother, I am unable to understand You and act accordingly. This is my greatest sorrow. How am I to understand You?"

---

[9] It is said that the chataka bird (the hornbill bird) will drink only raindrops that fall during the rains. It does not relish any other water. In the absence of rain, the chataka bird is thirsty and miserable.

Mother smiled and replied, "To understand Me, you have to become Me."

It was the same as if Balu had asked how he was to understand infinity. "Unless you become infinity, you cannot understand infinity," was the answer.

This is just one small incident. There have been countless incidents of this kind.

MOTHER'S ILLNESS

One morning Mother was found to be very ill. She was so weak that She couldn't even get up from Her bed. It happened to be a Sunday, and hundreds of people were waiting for Mother's morning *darshan*. She complained that She was having trouble breathing and that Her whole body was in terrible pain (Sometimes this happens when Mother takes upon Herself the diseases of devotees). She was in so much agony that She was rolling on the bed. But the single bed was not wide enough, so Mother decided that She wanted to lie on the bare floor. Gayatri and the brahmacharins were afraid that the cold floor would only aggravate her pain, so they spread a thick blanket over it. But Mother didn't want the blanket, so Gayatri removed it and she then helped Mother down onto the floor. As Mother lay on the bare floor, She began to roll back and forth groaning with pain. Her suffering was obvious. The brahmacharins decided that there should be no morning *darshan* or

Devi Bhava that day. They mentioned this to Mother, but Mother didn't say anything. Taking Her silence as consent, a sign was placed in front of the Ashram announcing the cancellation of both the morning *darshan* and Devi Bhava. One of the brahmacharins went downstairs and broke the news to the devotees who were waiting for Mother in the *darshan* hut. They were all greatly disappointed.

It was just after nine-thirty. Mother was still lying on the floor. Her physical condition had not improved even slightly. Everybody was feeling worried. Gayatri and Damayantiamma were massaging Mother's legs while a brahmacharini was holding a hot water bottle against Her chest. All eyes were fixed on Mother. All of a sudden Mother sprang up from the floor and asked, "What time is it?" Everyone was astonished and they all asked, "Why, Amma? Why do you want to know the time?" It sounded like a chorus.

"Why do you ask?" said Mother, as if nothing had happened, as if there had never been anything wrong with Her. "Why, don't you know that today is Sunday? The devotees must be waiting downstairs for *darshan*. What time is it?" She again inquired. She turned to look at the clock, and when She discovered what time it was She exclaimed, "Oh Shivane! It's nearly nine forty-five!" By now She was on Her feet. Br. Nealu protested and said, "But Amma, we have already announced that there will be no *darshan* today, and the devotees already know about it. They are slowly getting ready to go. Amma, you are very sick. You need to rest for at least one day." Mother gave Nealu a stern look and said, "What did you say? Did you say to them that there is no *darshan* today? Did you make such an announcement? And who told you that Amma is sick? Amma is not sick! She has never done any such thing before! Amma is surprised to see that you, who have been with Her for such a long time, are still so utterly lacking in compassion. How could you even think of sending all those devotees away?" She immediately sent Br. Pai downstairs to inform everyone that Mother would be giving *darshan* as usual. The devotees were elated and they all rushed back into the hut.

By now Mother looked completely normal. There was no sign of any pain or illness to be seen in Her at all. She said to the brahmacharins, "You do not understand the feelings of the devotees. Some of them have been waiting eagerly for a long time to see Amma. Many of them have had to borrow money, or sell their earrings or nose rings, to be able to come and see Amma. There are many who scrape together ten paise a day, from their meagre earnings, to save enough money for the bus fare to visit the Ashram once a month. It's easy for you to send them away, saying that there is no *darshan* today. But think of the mental agony that they will go through if they cannot see Amma. Think of all the trouble they have had to undergo to come here.

Think of their disappointment. Most of the devotees won't make any major decisions in their lives without first asking Amma. Those who are here now may need an answer today. There are certain things which cannot be postponed. How easy it was for you to suddenly decide that there would be no *darshan* today. Children, try to understand the problems of others and try to feel their sorrow."

Br. Nealu was concerned and remarked, "What will people think about us? They are going to think that we brahmacharins cancelled the *darshan* on our own initiative."

Mother again looked sternly at Nealu and said, "Nealu, are you still concerned about what people think about you? Very good! So you are afraid of others and their ill feelings. Whatever happened was Amma's wish - can't you take it in that way? Is this how a disciple should feel about his Master? The thought of what others may think about you comes from the ego. The ego wants a good image. You don't want anyone to dislike you or to criticize you. You are far more worried about that than feeling any concern about Amma's health. A surrendered person would never think like this. Once you have surrendered, you do not think about yourself or what others may think about you. You should learn to surrender your ego."

As soon as Mother had finished speaking, Gayatri requested everyone to leave the room, so that Mother could get ready for *darshan*.

A STRANGER TO FIX THE MIND

Twenty minutes later Mother came down to the *darshan* hut and began receiving the devotees. She looked enthusiastic and cheerful, and She was also looking perfectly healthy.

The brahmacharins once asked Mother how they were to understand these perplexing moods of Hers, and why She sometimes acted in such seemingly strange ways.

Mother answered, "It is only according to your strange and noisy mind that Amma is acting strangely. You feel that it is strange because you have certain preconceived ideas about behavior. You have picked up certain concepts and habits from your own life and from the way in which you have been brought up. You believe that certain ways of behavior are strange and that other ways are normal. Strangeness and normality are nothing but your own concepts, your own personal belief. You want Amma to speak and behave according to the way in which your mind has been trained.

"You may have certain ideas about life which you think are right, but they are bound to be different from everyone else's. Everyone has his own ideas, his own thoughts and feelings, and each one thinks that he is right and that everyone else is wrong. Everyone functions like this. Each mind has created its own concepts, and each mind expects Amma to fit within that framework.

"It is true that Amma is trying to please all Her devotees who come to Her to unburden their sorrows, their suffering and their fear. You must have seen how Amma behaves towards them to make them feel at ease, so that they will open up in Her presence. The more they open up, the more Amma can work on them. Amma would gladly sacrifice Her entire life for the sake of making others happy. But, Amma doesn't believe that She should treat you, who wish to devote your entire life to know God, in the same way. Your mind needs to be churned and churned, so that it will become clearer than the clearest - so transparent that you will be able to perceive your real existence, the Atman. In other words, you have to become mindless. But this is not easy. The mind cannot simply be removed. It is dissolved by the heat produced by *tapas*, and this heat is created by the Master's disciplining, coupled with your love and attachment towards him.

"Your mind and intellect cannot comprehend the Master, which is why you call him strange and contradictory. But understand that it is only your mind that judges him like that.

"In the heat produced by *tapas*, the mind, along with all its judgements and preoccupations, will melt away, and you begin to function from your heart. For this to happen the disciple must have a tremendous amount of patience.

"A true Master sacrifices his entire life for the uplift of his disciples, devotees and the entire society. But there also has to be a certain amount of commitment from the other end. Be patient and you will receive everything from the true Master.

"Don't try to judge the Master with your intellect. Your understanding of him is bound to be completely wrong. Because you dwell in the mind, and your habits and tendencies are very strong, you will insist on trying to solve the mystery of the Master's 'strange moods' through logic and reasoning. But you will fail to understand until, at last, it will be revealed to you that the Master cannot be understood through the mind or intellect. You will realize that faith alone is the way. It is only through surrender and a childlike openness that one can come to know him.

"In the process of trying to comprehend the Master through your intellect, your mind will become exhausted. You will realize that you are helpless in your efforts to understand the infinite nature of the Master with your intellect, and you finally open up. You suddenly become receptive. This process involves *tapas*, and it is your love and attachment to the Master's external form that extracts the heat.

"You may call the Master strange, but it is only according to your mind that he is strange. The mind creates a sense of strangeness in you because you identify with it. The more you surrender to the disciplining of the Master, with an intense feeling of love in your heart, the more you will come to know that it is your own mind that is strange, and not the Master.

"The mind is an outsider. He is a stranger in your real abode - the Self. The mind, being a foreign element, creates an irritation which itches. The itching is the desires of the mind. It is just like the sensation you sometimes get to scratch an itching wound. As you scratch the area, you find it soothing, and so you scratch it repeatedly until the wound and the surrounding area become red and infected. And with that, the pain of the wound increases.

"The mind creates such an itch when it is full of desires and emotions. So you keep on scratching, until finally, your whole life becomes a big pus infected wound.

"All that pus needs to be squeezed out of your wound; only then will the wound be healed. It is Amma's duty to treat the wound and squeeze out the pus. That is how Amma shows Her compassion towards you, but when She does, you call it strange. But Amma isn't bothered by your reaction, for it is only due to your lack of understanding. You would call Amma normal if She just kept on soothing the wound and allowed you to continue to scratch it. The choice is yours. If you want the wound only to be soothed and not healed, it is all right with Mother, but you will suffer later.

"Suppose you go to see a doctor to have a wound treated. The doctor might give you an injection, after which you may feel even more pain than before. The wound might become filled with pus and the pain may be excruciating. You ask the doctor, 'How can I be in so much pain when you have given me the medication?' The doctor smilingly replies, 'Don't worry. The injection was meant to bring out all the pus. It has to come out.' The doctor looks pleased about your condition, because he knows it means that the treatment is working. But you think it is strange that the doctor is pleased. You cannot blame the doctor for your limited understanding. He knows what he is doing, and it is his duty to do what is best for you. Don't judge the doctor. You are likely to misjudge him, because you do not know anything. He is healing the wound, but before the wound is healed, pain is unavoidable. The present pain you are experiencing is meant to remove all pain. If you yourself are not a doctor and you do not know anything about medical treatment, your ideas about how a disease should be treated belong to you and your mind alone.

"The same is the case with a true Master. Your sense of confusion and the pain that you have are due to the spiritual medication which he has given you, to bring out the pus from the wounds of your past.

"External cuts and wounds are not a big problem. They will soon heal, provided that they are treated properly. But the inner wounds are far more serious. They can destroy your entire life because you are ignorant and do not know anything about them. An ordinary doctor cannot treat such wounds. They are deep, age old wounds, for which you need an all-knowing, divine doctor. A real Master is absolutely necessary, someone who can see into all your past lives, who knows how to treat and cure your inner wounds."

Question: "Amma, You compared the mind to a foreign element. Why is it foreign? Could You please elaborate on this point?"

Mother: "Whenever a foreign element enters into our lives we ruthlessly try to reject it. For example, if there is a dust particle in our eye we want to remove it. Why? Because it is not part of the eye. It doesn't belong to us. What about an illness? Even if it is a headache or stomach ache we will want to get rid of it, because it is foreign to us. The body wants to reject it, for it is not part of our nature. Similarly, the mind is a foreign element, a complete stranger, that we need to get rid of.

"Everybody wants to be happy and peaceful. There are no arguments about that. But, to attain real peace and happiness one has to go beyond the mind and its desires. It is the mind that causes the sorrow and the itching. The mind is like a wound. Every time a desire crops up you feel an 'itching' sensation of the wound of the mind. Fulfilling the desire is like scratching the wound, and your itch is relieved for the moment. But you are completely unaware of the truth that by yielding to your desires, you are making the wound of the mind deeper. It becomes more and more infected. But the mind will constantly continue to demand and desire, and you will continue to fulfill those desires. It is like a continuous scratching of the wound of the mind, which only makes the wound increasingly larger.

"If you vigorously keep rubbing the dust in your eyes instead of removing it, your pain and irritation will only increase. Remove the dust and you will be all right. Similarly, the mind is like dust in the eye, a foreign element. Learn to get rid of the mind. Only then will you achieve perfection and happiness.

"To be happy and peaceful is the goal of all human beings. But they choose the wrong ways to attain it. Almost everyone knows that they are not experiencing real peace and happiness. They are lacking something in their lives and they try to fill that gap by acquiring and possessing. But the real problem exists within your mind. The mind is a stranger that needs to be eliminated. But who can do this? Only a complete stranger to your mind can eliminate it. The Master is that Stranger. The *Mahatma*, the Perfect Master, is perhaps incomprehensible to your mind, but he knows your strange mind and its strange ways perfectly well. He is the Master of all minds, but to your mind he is a very strange phenomenon indeed.

"As long as your mind exists, you will judge the *Mahatma's* ways as strange, but when you slowly start to control the mind and thoughts, you will realize that there was nothing strange at all about the *Mahatma*, it was only your mind that was strange.

"As Amma has mentioned before, your mind needs

to be churned. Only a certain stranger with strange moods knows how to churn your mind. You are used to ordinary people and their moods, and your mind sometimes gets churned by them. But this churning is only superficial and is not sufficient. The effect of real churning should reach the bottom most part of your mind; only then does purification take place. No ordinary individual can do this, because no ordinary person knows the strangeness of your mind as well as the true Master. A true Master is beyond the senses and the mind. That is why you call him strange. But only such a strange person who is beyond the mind and the senses can do the churning effectively, and help you to eliminate your strange mind and its strange feelings. That strange person is the Master - the Satguru. The Satguru brings the disciple close to him through his love and compassion, and then slowly, by his seemingly strange ways and moods, the churning begins.

"Children, there is a Malayalam proverb which says, 'Catch the fish after stirring up the water.' If you create turbulence in a pond, all the fish living in different parts of the pond will come out from beneath the mud and from other hiding places. They will hear the frightening noise and come scurrying out. It is like a total churning of the pond. Once all the fish have come out of their hiding places, the fisherman will cast his net and capture them. In a similar way, the Master will create turbulence in our minds, through his strange, incomprehensible ways. But this turbulence will bring out all the vasanas (tendencies) lying dormant deep within. Only if these vasanas manifest can we become aware of them and remove them. The Master's strange ways have been deliberately created only to catch your mind. The turbulence that the Master makes you experience is only to show you the amount of negativity that you have within. Once you realize the tremendous weight of the burden of negativity that you are carrying, you will have a sincere desire to get rid of it. This will enable you to cooperate with the Master, because now you know the root-cause of the itching; you know how deep the wound is. You don't want to carry the burden anymore. You want to unburden yourself and be completely happy and relaxed. Once you become aware of the negativity, it will be easy to eliminate it. You come to know that your mind is the real cause of all your sorrow and suffering, and you will be able to renounce it, by the Grace of the Master."

CHAPTER TEN

A GOOD REMINDER

*O*ne brahmacharin wanted to leave the Ashram for a few months and spend some time in solitude. He had been asking Mother about this for some time. But Mother said to him, "Why do you want to go? Is it going to do you any good? Amma doesn't think that you would gain anything by being away from this atmosphere. If your goal is Self-Realization, this is the best place to be. But, if you want to act according to your *vaṣanas*, then it's fine, go ahead. It is your mind that is the problem. As long as you carry the mind along with you wherever you go, you are not going to gain anything. You can keep on changing places and situations, but you will remain the same old person with the same old habits and tendencies, unless you stop your noisy mind. Self-Realization will remain out of reach for you until you silence your mind. What you need is not another place or situation, but a person who has completely silenced his own mind. Only such a person can help you become aware of your real problem and bring you out of it; only such a person can help your mind become still and silent."

The brahmacharin nevertheless decided to go. He left the Ashram early one morning, leaving a letter for

Mother, saying, "Amma, forgive me for disobeying You. The desire to be alone is so strong that I cannot resist it. I simply have to leave. Oh Compassionate One, please accept me as Your son and disciple when I return."

But the brahmacharin, who had wanted to be in solitude for at least three months, returned to the Ashram that same day. He later described a very interesting incident which forced him to give up the idea of leaving the Ashram.

Hoping to catch the early morning bus to Kayamkulam, he had taken a boat across the backwaters and was about to proceed to the bus stop, when all of a sudden, half a dozen dogs ran up right in front of him and stood blocking his way. The brahmacharin thought that the dogs were harmless, so he decided to ignore them and tried to move forward. But as soon as he moved, the dogs began to bark at him and they looked fierce. The brahmacharin grabbed a stick which was lying nearby, intending to use it to frighten the dogs away. But this move enraged the dogs and their barking became ferocious. Some of the dogs moved threateningly close to the brahmacharin. He had wanted to frighten the dogs away, but finally he himself became so frightened that he let go of the stick. As soon as he dropped the stick, the dogs stopped barking and stood still, but they were not yet willing to give up. They continued to block his way and wouldn't move an inch.

The brahmacharin made a second and third attempt to proceed to the bus stop, but whenever he tried to take a step forward, the dogs began to bark again, as they continued to block his way.

At one point the brahmacharin got so angry with the dogs that he took a few threatening steps toward them. But as he did so, one of the dogs jumped at him, and with a lightning move, bit him on the calf of his right leg. It wasn't a deep wound but his leg was bleeding. The brahmacharin was shocked at what had just happened. It was, in fact, an eye opener for him. He thought, "This must be Mother's *leela*, because She doesn't want me to go. I am being disobedient, but not even my disobedience will succeed if it isn't Mother's will. Why else would these dogs act in such a strange way?" Thinking in this way and feeling somewhat consoled, the brahmacharin returned to the Ashram.

The brahmacharin wanted to keep this incident a secret. He decided to tell Mother about it at a later time, when he got an opportunity. But, to his wonderment, the next morning Mother asked him, "The dogs taught you a lesson, didn't they?" Mother laughed and continued, "Son, let this serve as a fitting punishment for your disobedience." Everybody soon found out about the incident. During the next two days, as the brahmacharin was walking around the Ashram with a bandage on his leg, he aroused a lot of laughter wherever he went, and was teased mercilessly by the other residents. Looking at his bandage, Mother laughed and said, "Let this serve as a good reminder." The brahmacharin was full of remorse. He shed copious tears asking Mother to forgive him.

Later he wanted to know how this could have happened. He asked Mother, "Why did the dogs behave in such a strange way? It was Your will that was being expressed through them, wasn't it? But is such a thing possible?"

THE ALL-PERVASIVE NATURE
OF A TRUE MASTER

Mother replied, "Son, haven't you heard the story about how all of Nature answered when the great sage Vedavyasa called his son, Suka, urging him to come back? Even as a boy, Suka was detached from the world. Vedavyasa wanted his son to get married and lead the normal life of a householder. But Suka, who was born divine, was strongly inclined to live the life of a renunciate. So, one day he gave up everything and left to become a *sannyasin*. While Suka was walking away, Vedavyasa called out his son's name. It was Nature that responded to his call - the trees, the plants, the mountains, valleys, animals and birds - they all answered him. But what exactly does this mean?

"A person who has become one with the Supreme Consciousness is also one with all of creation. He is no longer just the body. He is the life force which shines in and through everything in creation. He is that Consciousness which lends its beauty and vitality to everything. He is the Self, which is immanent in everything. This is the meaning of the story.

"When Vedavyasa called his son, Suka, Nature answered, because Suka was that Pure Consciousness which is immanent in all of Nature. Vedavyasa called Suka, but Suka was not the body and therefore had no name or form. He was beyond name and form. He existed within everyone, and the bodies of all creatures were his. He was in every body, and therefore everything responded.

"You saw only the bodies of the dogs. But what was within those bodies? Within each body dwells the Atman. You may call what you see a dog because it has a dog's body. But once you realize the truth, you will experience that the dog and everything that exists in creation is pervaded by the Supreme Atman. A true *Mahatma* can make anything obey him, whether it be sentient or insentient. Everything is his, everything can be controlled by him. Nothing is impossible for a *Mahatma*. Even a wooden plank will do anything he wishes it to do. What then can't he ask a dog to do, who is far more intelligent! The *Mahatma* can act through the sun, the moon, the ocean, mountains, trees and animals. He can express himself through the entire universe. He just has to give the command. A word, a glance, a thought or a touch is enough to make anything obey.

"Do you know the story of how Sri Krishna turned the entire herd of cows against a powerful demon who came to steal the herd? He turned the cows against the demon by simply playing the flute. The demon was a servant of Kamsa, Krishna's evil uncle. Kamsa had tried many different methods to kill Krishna, using his faithful demons, one after the other, to do the job. But all his attempts had failed. His frequent failures made Kamsa very revengeful. One day, he called another demon and ordered him to kill all the cows belonging to Krishna and his friends.

"Every morning Krishna and the cowherd boys used to take the cows to the meadows to graze. The meadows were far away from Gokul, where Krishna and His friends lived. One day, when the cows were grazing happily in a forest, the demon appeared. He first of all wanted to take all the cows to a more suitable place where he could use his demonic powers to kill them. The hideous appearance of the demon was enough to frighten the cows, and they ran hither and thither in a frenzy. The demon managed to gather the whole herd and make them run in a particular direction. Krishna's friends, the cowherd boys, were terrified and they rushed to the place where Sri Krishna was sitting. When they told Him what had happened, Sri Krishna smiled, whereupon He took out His flute and began to play a beautiful, melodious tune. That was all that was needed. As soon as they heard that melodious tune, the cows, who were running in the direction towards which the demon was chasing them, turned around and began to chase the demon. There were hundreds of cows, and now the demon's magical powers had no effect on them at all. So finally, it was the demon who was forced to flee from the cows.

"The Saint, Jnaneswar, could make a wall move and a bullock chant the *Vedas*.

"Mastery over the mind means mastery over all of creation. It does not mean only the mastery over your own individual mind. You become the master of all minds, all minds are under your command. You are the whole, and not the part. Once you realize this, there can be no separation from anything."

TAKE REFUGE AT THE FEET
OF A PERFECT MASTER

In connection with the incident of the brahmacharin who tried to leave, Mother later elaborated, "People all over the world run here and there, in search of spirituality and Self-Realization. They want to find a peaceful, solitary place, perhaps a cave, or a forest, or a mountainous area, with a river running nearby, and so on. What they should do first of all is learn how to become patient and settle down somewhere - but not just anywhere they like; it should be at the feet of a person who can help them to see that their problems do not stem from somewhere outside themselves, but that they exist within. It should be someone who can take the seeker by the hand and lead him to the goal; it should be someone who will make the aspirant feel that he is not alone - that he will always have the help and loving guidance of his Master, who is endowed with infinite spiritual power.

"This is not an easy path, and there is pain involved. But, the aspirant should not feel too much pain, for then he may fall from the path or he may want to run away. Competent students are hard to find nowadays. They existed a long time ago, when truth and faith were prevalent in society. Their intent on the goal was so strong that they could easily withstand the strict disciplining of the Master. Those seekers had complete faith and self-surrender. But things have changed. Faith and self-surrender have become limited to words. More speaking and less doing is the policy of the modern age, and the tendencies of the mind are stronger than before. No one wants to be disciplined. Everyone wants to keep their ego, it is so precious to them. People think that the ego is an embellishment; it is not considered to be a burden anymore. People do not feel the heaviness of their ego. They feel comfortable inside its small, hard shell. They feel afraid and insecure to come out of it. They think that they are well protected where they are. For them, what lies beyond the shell of their ego is frightening, it is unknown and therefore unsafe.

They believe that what lies beyond their ego is not for them, it is meant only for those who are 'not capable of doing anything else.'

IT TAKES COURAGE TO SURRENDER

"Surrendering to a Master is not easy. It needs courage. It is like jumping into a flowing river. The Master is the flowing river. Once you jump in, the current will inexorably take you to the sea. There is no escape. You may struggle and try to swim against the current, but the river is so strong that it is bound to take you to the ocean - to God, or the Self - your real dwelling place. To jump in is to surrender. It needs a courageous mind because it can be compared to the death of your body and mind.

"You may not take the plunge now, because you are not yet ready to jump into the deep waters of the river. For the time being, you may want to remain standing on the river bank enjoying the beauty of the river. You may want to enjoy the cool gentle breeze, the constant chatter of the running water, the power and charm of the river. That is fine. The river is not going to force you to jump in, and you can stand there for as long as you like because it won't send you away. It is not going to say, 'Enough is enough! Go away! There is a long waiting list.' Nor is it going to say, 'Okay, the time has come. You either jump into me right now, or I will force you.' No, nothing of the sort. It is all up to you.

You can either jump in or stay on the shore. The river is simply there. It is always willing to accept you and to cleanse you.

"The river of the Master does not have an ego. It does not think, 'I am flowing, I am powerful and beautiful. I have the power to take you to the ocean. In fact, I am the ocean. See how many people bathe and swim in me, and how they find delight in me!' No, the river of the Master has no such feelings. It just flows because its nature is to do so.

"But once you dive in, the current is such that you will become almost like a corpse. You will find yourself so powerless, that you have no other choice but to simply be still and let the river carry you wherever it wants. You have the freedom to choose. You can either remain on the shore or dive in. But once you take the leap, you do not have a choice anymore; you will lose your individuality, you will have to give up your ego. At that point you disappear and you find that you are floating in Pure Consciousness.

"So, you are free to stay on the shore. But for how long? Sooner or later, you will either have to turn and go back to the world, or you will have to jump. Even if you return to the world, the beauty and charm of the river is so enchanting and so tempting that you will keep on coming back. The day will come when you will be tempted to take that final leap. And finally you will dive in - it has to happen.

"While standing on the shore you may have many things to say about the river. You will sing its praises, you will describe its beauty, you will have many opinions about it, and you have unending stories to tell about the river and its history. But you are describing the river and telling stories about it without having taken a dip in it even once. And whatever you may say about the greatness of the river without having gone into it, is simply meaningless. Once you finally dive in, once you surrender to the River of Existence - the Perfect Master - you will be silent. You will have nothing to say.

"Surrender makes you silent. Surrender destroys the ego and helps you to experience your nothingness and God's omniscience. Once you know that you are nothing, that you are totally ignorant, then you have nothing to say. You have only unconditional and undivided faith; you can only bow down in utmost humility. In order to really know, one should be humble. The ego and real knowledge are not compatible. Humility is the sign of true knowledge.

"There are people who are good speakers. They tend to have big egos. There are exceptions, but the general tendency is to speak more and do less. Why? Because they haven't surrendered to a higher reality, to the higher values of life. They have not really accepted God's all-powerful nature and become aware of their own nothingness, even though they may speak about it. Such people may do a lot of good for the world, but they also do a lot of harm.

"Amma is not trying to generalize. Everyone is not like that. There are people among them who have surrendered, but they are only a few who can be counted on one's finger tips. The general tendency is to be as egoistic as possible.

THE EGO KILLS THE REAL YOU

"The greatest problem with the world of politics and business is the tough competition, the tug of war which goes on between party members or rival business groups, as each one tries to establish its supremacy over the others. In situations like that you have to show some aggression towards your rivals; you want to gain power over them, and you therefore need to show them that you count for something. To achieve your goal, you are willing to use any method. You do not even care if it is inhuman. And in the struggle to survive you lose your qualities as a human being. You become almost like an animal. You lose your heart and a hard rock takes its place. Your concern for your fellow beings will be lost. The real you will be sacrificed. Amma has heard a story.

"A man was involved in a lawsuit. He thought he might lose the case and desperately told his lawyer that he was about to send the judge an entire set of golf clubs, as a bribe. The lawyer was shocked and said to his client, 'The judge takes great pride in his honesty. He cannot be bribed. If you do that, it will only serve to turn him against you and then you can just imagine the result.'

The man won the case, and when it was all over he invited his lawyer for dinner. He expressed his gratitude towards the lawyer for his advice concerning the golf clubs. 'I did, in fact, send them to the judge,' he said, 'but I sent them on behalf of our opponent.'

"The ego makes life very similar to a battle field, and in a battlefield there are only enemies, there are no friends, no near or dear ones. In a battlefield there is no love or concern for others. You are always thinking about how to destroy the other. You never even consider forgetting and forgiving. Even those who seem to be on your side are trying to pull you down. In fact, they are thinking the same way that you are. They have similar suspicions. And so it is, that to begin with, you destroy the people on the opposite side, and then you end up destroying the people on your own side. Power and money make you blind. Why should there be all this trouble? Because there is no surrender or humility. Everybody feels that they are something special, that they are great. So, they keep trying to show others how great they are, and this is what always ends in destruction.

"The other day, a film actor visited Amma and talked

about his struggle for survival in the film business. He said to Amma, 'People are of the impression that the film business is one of the best fields of work, and that film stars live happy and contented lives.' With great pain he told Amma that the film business is one of the worst professions you can be involved in, because of all the jealousy and competitiveness which exists between actors. Those who are at the top never encourage the other actors to succeed. Even though there are many talented actors and actresses, they are at the mercy of producers, directors and the leading actors and actresses. There is a shameless hostility among them, as each one tries to pull the others down.

"Sometimes people hide their egos to achieve something. Suppose a person wants to find a job. He has been wandering around for a long time, unable to find any work. As he approaches a factory owner asking for a job, he carefully hides his ego and pretends to be very humble. He readily agrees to all the conditions that the owner puts forth, and he signs the contract. He even repeats a pledge several times, saying that he will never participate in any kind of strike or protest which might be instigated against the management, and that he will discharge his duties promptly, without fail. But once the job is his, he begins to think that he is something and he wants to show it. He begins to break all his promises and he forgets about the pledge that he repeated. He brings his ego out from hiding.

"When you surrender to a higher consciousness, you give up all your claims; you release your grip from everything that you've been holding on to. Whether you gain or lose, it doesn't matter now. You don't want to be something any longer. You long to be nothing, absolutely nothing. So you dive into the River of Existence.

"The ego, or the mind, is that which makes you feel that you are something. Unless it is eliminated, you cannot dive deep into your own consciousness. You have to become nothing. Not even a trace of, 'I am something' should remain. If you are something, there is no entry into the realm of Pure Consciousness.

BEAUTY LIES IN EGOLESSNESS

"The ego can only destroy. It destroys everything - even life itself. It destroys everything that is good and beautiful. When the ego is predominant, ugliness is also predominant, because the ego is inherently ugly and repulsive. An egoistic person may be considered handsome and highly capable, but there will nevertheless be an unpleasant feeling about him.

"Ravana, the demon king, was handsome, majestic and very talented. He was a great singer and musician. He could play several instruments beautifully at the same time. He was a great scholar, a great composer and writer. But there was always something abhorrent

about him. Even though he had all these great qualities, he also had a disagreeable nature. This was because he was extremely egotistic. He thought he was
greater than everybody else. The thought that, 'I am
something great,' creates a certain ugliness in people.

"Vedavyasa, on the other hand was not at all handsome. But his presence was divine and exceptionally
beautiful because he was the very embodiment of humility and simplicity. He had no ego. He was genu-
inely great, but he never claimed that he was great in
any way. He thought of himself as being nothing, and
because of this, he was everything.

"Vedavyasa was a completely surrendered soul; whereas
Ravana had not surrendered at all. Ravana had a grossly
inflated ego; whereas Vedavyasa had no individual ego
at all. He was Pure Consciousness personified. The
difference is enormous."

Everybody sat spellbound as they listened to Mother's
words. They kept gazing at Mother - the incomprehensible One.

Br. Pai sang a song called, *Ammayennullora Ten
Mori.*

> *Is there one other name*
> *among the countless names in existence*
> *that equals the honey-like name of Amma?*
> *Is there any realm*
> *other than the one of Your Love*

that is worthy of being the resting place
for all my thoughts?

O Mother, if you forsake this helpless one
who is wandering
along the shores of lonely nights,
then the garden of my mind
will be haunted by endless sorrows.

Oh Mother, is there anyone, except You
my only support
who knows my innermost sorrows?
If we who adore You
should become a despicable lot
what purpose would there be
in meditating on Your Lotus Feet?

O blessed, infinite Light
Please caress me with the slightest touch
of Your glance.
If You do, my mind will flow
along the sacred River
of Nectarous Bliss.

CHAPTER ELEVEN

*D*uring the Devi Bhava one evening, Br. Balu couldn't sing because he had a sore throat. So, he sat inside the temple, meditating and repeating his mantra, and often simply gazing at Mother's radiant face.

Saumya was sitting at Mother's other side, serving Her as she did during every Bhava *darshan*. In the beginning Gayatri and Saumya were the only brahmacharinis who were staying permanently at the Ashram. Before that, in the early days, when the Krishna and Devi Bhavas first began, it was the local women devotees who served Mother during each Bhava *darshan*. When Gayatri came to stay permanently, in the beginning of 1980, she began taking care of Mother's personal needs, and she also started serving Mother during the Divine Moods. The task of serving Mother during Bhava *darshan* was later passed on to Saumya, when she became a permanent resident at the end of 1982.

It was a common practice in those days for Mother to let one of the brahmacharins sit right next to Her, on Her left side, during Devi Bhava. Those were very precious moments.

Having invited a brahmacharin to sit close to Her, Mother would usually apply some sandal paste between his eyebrows. This touch had a wonderful effect on the recipient; it created a feeling of such tremendous peace that he would spontaneously become absorbed in deep meditation. She therefore deliberately bestowed this blessing upon them. The first group of brahmacharins were very fortunate to receive this experience. There were times when one of them would be called to come and sit next to Mother and She would let him lay his head on Her lap. While lying with his head on Mother's lap he would have wonderful visions and other spiritual experiences. It was, of course, considered to be a great privilege and blessing to be allowed to sit next to Mother during Devi Bhava. Occasions were not few when Mother bestowed this blessing upon a householder devotee.

As being allowed to sit next to Mother during Devi Bhava was considered an expression of Her special love, each brahmacharin always waited anxiously for Mother to call him. But among the six or seven brahmacharins who were then living at the Ashram, Mother would invite only one of them to sit next to Her during each Devi Bhava. On some days She completely ignored the brahmacharins and asked a householder devotee to come and sit next to Her. When the others realized that they had lost their chance for this time, they would become extremely jealous of the chosen one. But, in due course, Mother completely stopped this practice of calling one of them.

The memories of those days still remain fresh and vivid among the brahmacharins. The deep, spontaneous meditations that they used to experience on those occasions were extraordinary. Sometimes Mother would also take the time to answer the questions of the person who sat next to Her.

This was one such blessed night for Br. Balu.

On the front veranda of the temple, *bhajans* were being sung with great intensity. Br. Pai was singing *Oru Pidi Sneham*.

> *I have wandered after shadows*
> *yearning for a morsel of Love*
> *But, when almost within grasp*
> *Love slipped from my hand.*
> *Oh Mother, here I am*
> *wandering again*
> *O Mother.*
>
> *My heart is broken*
> *struck by the lashing waves*
> *of grief.*
> *O Mother*
> *Where is this shattered soul*
> *to search for You?*
> *Do You not care?*
> *O Mother, do You not care?*
>
> *As I continuously drink*
> *the tears of sorrow,*

I shall sleep no more.
O Mother, have mercy on me
so that I may reawaken
and discover myself
at Your Lotus Feet.

Balu was sitting next to the wall, at a slight distance from Mother. He was gazing at Mother's beautiful countenance, and he was thinking to himself, "How wonderful it would be if Mother were to call me now and let me sit close to Her." Suddenly Mother looked at him and smilingly invited him to come and sit beside Her. Balu's happiness knew no bounds. The thought that Mother had responded to his prayer so quickly, made him feel completely open and receptive.

Without wasting a moment, Balu moved closer to Mother and sat on the floor next to Her *peetham*. Mother looked at him with a beaming smile and said, "Amma knew that you had an intense desire to sit next to Her." Balu fixed his gaze on Mother's face and shed silent tears. When Mother saw this, Her compassion towards Her child overflowed, and She expressed this by gently putting Balu's head on Her lap. And as She kept his head cradled in Her lap, She continued to give *darshan* to the devotees.

From the temple veranda, Pai could be heard reciting the following *Amritanandamayi Stavamanjari* sloka as an introduction to a song:

I prostrate before You, O Mother
Who is the Essence of Aum
the Infinite, the Eternal
Existence-Knowledge-Bliss, Absolute
that shines in the temple of the hearts of Sages...

Who brings joy
to upright and steadfast disciples
immersed in meditation...

Who instills in them
the fervent devotion
that arises from soulful devotional singing...

the Mother, who is adored
by those who are virtuous.

Balu lifted his head from Mother's lap and once again looked at Mother's radiant face. As She threw a compassionate glance at him, Balu asked Her, "Amma, have I been with You in all Your previous incarnations?"

Mother smiled and replied, "Son, you have always been with Amma. Son, know that all those who are with Amma now were with Her in all Her previous incarnations. Otherwise, how could you feel this strong and spontaneous bond with Her?"

Question: "Amma, some say that it is the Guru who chooses the disciple; others say that the disciple chooses the Guru. Which is correct? Did You choose me or did I choose You? Did I find You or did You find me? Could You please clarify this?"

Mother: "Son, if Amma were to tell you that She chose you, would you believe it completely and blindly, without any doubts? No, Amma doesn't think so. In your present state you may believe it for a little while, but it won't take long before the mind starts raising its objections. It will apply the theory of cause and effect, and once that line of thinking is adopted, you will begin to analyze, thinking, 'Okay, so Amma said that it was She who found me. But, if She found me, it must have been the effect of something. What, then, is the cause? The cause must be my *punya* (merit) or the *tapas* that I have performed.' If you think in that way, the ego will slowly come crawling in.

"This may all seem very logical, but the best attitude for your spiritual growth would sound like this: 'God chose me. My Master chose me. I was lost and I was found by my Master, my All-in-all.'"

Question: "Will I attain Self-Realization in this lifetime or will I have to be born again for that?"

Mother: "Son, will you be able to put forth enough effort to destroy your mind and all your desires in this lifetime? Amma will always be by your side, to guide you and to hold your hand. But will you be able to do your *sadhana* regularly without fail, as Amma tells you to do? If you can do this, it is Amma's assumption that you will not be born again.

"Son, if you do your spiritual practices exactly as Amma instructs, you will definitely attain the state of

Self-Realization in three years. Amma can guarantee this. Then there will be no coming back. But the mind should disappear; the ego should die. If even a trace of the mind is left without being eliminated, you will have to come back."

Question: "Amma, I am not afraid of coming back. I just want to be with You, even if I have to take many more births!"

Mother: "Son, if you really are with Amma during this lifetime, you will definitely be with Her in all Her future incarnations. There is no doubt about it."

Question: "Amma, what do You mean by 'if you really are with Amma'? Aren't I with You now?"

Mother: "Unconditional obedience to Amma is what it means to 'really be with Her.' Being in Amma's physical presence, without being aware of the spiritual principles which She stands for, is not really being with Her - it is forgetting Her. Real remembrance of Amma is to obey Her words and to understand the spiritual import of those words, and to practice them. However, being in a *Mahatma's* presence will cause purification to take place of its own accord."

Balu looked up at Mother and said, "Amma, one last prayer. Bless me so that I may always be in Your Divine Presence."

Mother dipped Her index finger into a small bowl of sandal paste. She then placed the tip of Her finger between Balu's eyebrows and Balu felt immensely blissful. He closed his eyes, and as Mother continued to press Her finger against his third eye, he became absorbed in a state of deep meditation.

The brahmacharins were singing a song called *Brahmanda Pakshikal.*

> *O Mother*
> *You are the glorious Tree of Knowledge*
> *The galaxies fly to You*
> *like flocks of birds*
> *Until I reach You*
> *through the knowledge of my Self*
> *let me grow in Your shade.*

> *O Mother of Supreme Power*
> *I worship You*
> *knowing that the blue sky*
> *is Your head*
> *the earth is Your Feet*
> *and the whole atmosphere*
> *is Your body.*

> *O Mother*
> *who is glorified in all religions*
> *who is the Essence of the four Vedas*
> *and the Abode*
> *into which all names and forms*
> *finally dissolve*
> *I prostrate before You*
> *with all humility.*

At the end of the Devi Bhava, Mother called Dattan, the leper, to come up to Her for *darshan*. It was very touching and at the same time awe inspiring to see how Mother took care of him. He was given far more time and attention than any of the others.

Dattan went up to Mother and lay prostrate at Her feet. Mother raised him up and put his head on Her lap. After some time She gently lifted his head and held him against Her shoulder. She then began to lick his festering wounds with Her tongue. Such an extreme act of compassion can hardly be imagined. For those who witnessed what was taking place, it was both horrifying and deeply moving at the same time. One devotee who was standing in the temple fainted at the sight and had to be carried out of there. Mother then asked the rest of the devotees to leave the temple. What She did next was astounding. She made Dattan bend his head down, and holding his head between Her hands, She bit into a deeply infected wound on his forehead, and after having sucked out the blood and pus from it, She spat it out into a basin which Bri. Saumya held out next to Her. After repeating this scene a few more times, She took some sacred ash and rubbed it over the leper's body. Mother hugged him one more time with great affection, and finally walked over to the open doors of the temple and began to shower the devotees with flower petals, which marked the end of the Devi Bhava. It should also be mentioned here, that

Dattan was completely cured. His only medicine was Mother's saliva. All his wounds disappeared and only the scars remained on his body.

CHAPTER TWELVE

NOT MY RIGHT BUT HIS GRACE

*I*t was the day after Devi Bhava, and the Ashram was therefore less crowded. Balu, Venu, Ramakrishnan, Rao, Srikumar and Pai[10] were sitting next to Mother, who had just come down from Her room, and was sitting in front of the meditation hall. Balu took the opportunity to ask, "Amma, last night during Devi Bhava, when I asked You whether it is the disciple who chooses the Master or the Master who chooses the disciple, You said that it is always good for the spiritual growth of the disciple to have the attitude that, 'God has chosen me,' or 'My Master has chosen me.' Can you tell us a little more about this attitude?"

Mother: "Son, if you think that you were the one who chose your Master, it will make you feel egoistic. You cannot choose your Master unless he wants you to. It would be conceited to think, 'I have chosen my Mas-

---

[10]Balu is today known as Swami Amritaswarupananda,
Venu = Swami Pranavamritananda,
Ramakrishnan = Swami Ramakrishnananda,
Rao = Swami Amritatmananda, Srikumar = Swami Purnamritananda,
Pai = Swami Amritamayananda.

ter.' Then you could also abandon him whenever you wish. But how could you possibly choose your Master who is completely beyond your understanding? Before you choose or reject anything, you try to understand if it is good or bad for you. If it is good you choose it, otherwise you don't. You can also use it for some time and then get rid of it whenever you wish. There is a lot of thinking involved in that kind of choosing. But, whenever a disciple falls helplessly in love with the Master, at first sight, there is no thinking process involved. The Master's spiritual attraction is so great that the disciple becomes his. Thinking is an obstruction to real love and self-surrender.

"The Master, however, is not a thing, nor is he a limited person. The true Master is your very own Self, the Self of everything. He is infinity.

"How can the river choose the ocean? It flows helplessly towards the ocean. All rivers are like that: they are carried away towards the ocean and they merge with it. The pull of the ocean is so infinitely powerful that the rivers just have to flow in that direction.

"Similarly, you are helplessly being pulled towards the Supreme Master. His infinite power attracts you and so you flow towards him. The power of the Master precludes any choice on your part. The power is his alone. It is his Grace for which you cannot take any credit, whatsoever.

"You are just a tiny bit of iron filing which is helplessly being attracted towards the all-powerful magnet of the Master's spiritual glory. An iron filing has no choice. Once it is within the magnetic force of the magnet, it cannot choose whether to come or go. As the magnet draws it, it simply has to move in that direction. Similarly, you are being helplessly drawn towards the Supreme Master, and you have no choice. It just happens.

"The Master picks you out of the dirt and uplifts you to the same state in which he himself is constantly dwelling. Therefore, the right attitude is to think, 'I didn't choose him. He chose me.' But there is also a danger in thinking that you have been chosen by your Master, because then you will slowly start to feel, 'I am the chosen one. So, I must be special in some way.' This too is dangerous, because with that sort of attitude you easily forget about the part that the Master's Grace plays in all of this. You may think that because your Master wanted you, it is your absolute right to be his disciple, and this can easily inflate your ego. The ego of a spiritual person is far more subtle than the ego of a person who is leading a worldly life.

"It is much better if you think , 'It is only because of my Master's Grace that I am here with him. It is not my right. It is his gift. It was the Master who found me. I was useless, I was completely lost and without hope, but due to his Grace and compassion I am here now. I don't deserve anything, but he is showering me with his divine Grace anyway." This attitude will make you humble, and is very helpful in eradicating the ego. The most important thing is to constantly retain this awareness. As the mind and the pull of the *vasanas* are very powerful, it is easy to fall prey to them and forget about the Master's Grace. To become humble is the very goal of spiritual life. Humility alone is the way to God. On the other hand, if you feel that you were chosen by your Master, you may soon start thinking, 'There are so many people in the world, and yet my Master chose *me*. I must have acquired a lot of merit or spiritual power in my previous life. That must be why he chose me and no one else. No one, except me, is capable of doing the work that I am doing in this world. He wanted me and that is why I am here.'

"Such thoughts can overwhelm you and soon you become worse than anybody else. You will have a huge ego, and this is dangerous. Such an attitude will make you feel very self-important. Your personality will be disfigured by your ego. A true devotee or disciple will have great humility and because of this he will also possess a certain spiritual beauty. The beauty of spirituality lies in humility.

"The Master chooses you in order to save you. The fact that he has chosen you should be considered as a gift, which you don't actually deserve. It is not your right - it is his grace and his blessing. If you do not have this attitude, the ego will crawl in, without you even knowing it.

"One should have the humility to think, 'I am nothing. You are everything.' Only when you feel that you are nothing will you become everything. If you feel that you are something you will be nothing.

BEWARE OF THE SUBTLE EGO

Question: "Amma, You said that the ego of a spiritual person is very subtle and that it may even push us back into the world. Could You please explain this?"
Mother: "Children, just the thought, 'I am spiritual, I am spiritually advanced,' or 'I am a renunciate,' can be a big stumbling block to your spiritual progress. Such thoughts are also part of the ego, but a more subtle form of ego. You may think, 'I am great because I have renounced everything. Look at all those worldly people out there who are still immersed in the quagmire of materialism. They are so ignorant!' You may feel that those who live in the world are far beneath you. If you cherish such thoughts, it only shows that you are mentally immature. It means that you are ignorant. Those who live in the world may be ignorant, but they are not on the spiritual path; whereas, you are supposed to be on the spiritual path and yet you are still spiritually ignorant. Such thoughts are of the ego and need to be uprooted. If you are under the guidance of a real Master, you cannot feel this sort of pride. The Master will

immediately notice your pride and uproot it. A subtle ego is much more powerful and harder to destroy.

"A worldly person is proud of his achievements in life and likes to show them off. His ego is born out of his attachment to the objects of the external world. He has a big, beautiful house which he is attached to and feels very proud of. The house is excellent food for his ego. He is also proud of his power, wealth and reputation, and he sometimes expresses this on a large scale. You can experience it in his presence, even the way he walks and talks will have a certain air of pride about it. The more wealth and power you have, the more ego you will have. Whether you are wealthy or poor, the difference in ego lies only in degree.

"Also, the more thoughts you have, the more ego you will have. This is why scholars, thinkers and speakers are often more egotistic than others. People who enjoy a high position in society are often very egotistical, unless they have an attitude of self-surrender. They are used to being praised by the public, for the exceptional work that they are doing. Usually, the more famous you are, the more egotistic you are, because the ego grows with all the recognition. This is what happens to many people who are successful in the world. In such people, the ego is quite obvious; you will recognize it by their speech and by their actions. They cannot hide it; they are so full of ego that there is nowhere for their egos to hide. However, there are also people who have achieved fame and recognition, and yet they have remained humble. These are rare exceptions.

"It is quite natural for people who lead a materialistic life to be egoistic. It is pardonable, because they don't have the proper spiritual understanding. This is not the case with spiritual people who have dedicated their lives solely for that purpose. It has to be their way of life. They are supposed to be humble and devoid of any ego.

"Unfortunately, it may happen that a spiritual person learns how to hide his ego and pretends to be very humble. He tries not to show that he has an ego, because he knows that expressing it outwardly is wrong so far as a spiritual seeker is concerned. He knows that people won't appreciate it. It is also like this in the world, but there is a difference. In the world, once you are recognized as an expert in some field, the country needs you and you can afford to be egoistic. You can speak and act selfishly, but you are safe because of your expertise. Your employers, or those who have appointed you, cannot simply throw you out, unless they have a very good substitute. But in spiritual life it is not this way. Your spiritual advancement is recognized by the humility, egolessness and wisdom that you express.

"If a so-called spiritual person behaves in a very egoistic way, he will not be respected by people. He will only acquire a bad reputation within the spiritual

community. Knowing this, you will learn to suppress
your anger and all other negative tendencies, and you
act and behave like a spiritually mature person. This
becomes far too mental and subtle. As long as you express
it outwardly, it exists on a gross level. But when you
consciously keep it hidden within and act differently
on the outside, it becomes subtle and very dangerous.

"You can express your ego outwardly. That, too, can
be harmful, but it is less so, because at least people will
not be deluded. They will realize that you are egoistic
and be warned that you may harbor a lot of anger,
hatred, and other negative feelings within you. They
can then be careful of you and keep their distance, if
need be. But what if you skillfully learn how to hide
your ego and pretend to be a yogi? People will then be
seriously deluded, and that would amount to real cheat-
ing. But such hypocrisy cannot last. It cannot be hidden for long because soon, your ego will begin to expose
itself. What is hidden within must become manifest
sooner or later, no matter how much one may try to do
otherwise. It is just a question of time.

"It is like a mother-in-law with her newly arrived
daughter-in-law.[11] She will give her son's wife a lot of
love and attention in the beginning. She will not allow
her daughter-in-law to work in the kitchen, or to clean
the house or do any work outside, as if she were a

---

[11] In India it is customary for a newly wed couple to go and live with
the husband's family.

precious stone which would wear away if it is used too much. The mother-in-law can be heard telling her, 'My daughter, don't even think of such things! There are many others in the house who can do the work. Just sit down and relax.' When the oldest son's wife hears her mother-in-law say such things to the new-comer, she smiles to herself, for she knows from experience that it is just a big show; she knows that her mother-in-law will soon start showing her real nature. And this is exactly what happens. Within a week or two, the same mother-in-law, who until now has been so loving and concerned about her new daughter-in-law, can be heard shouting at her, 'You lazy girl! Do you think you are the master of this house? We are not your servants! Go and clean the kitchen!' This sort of thing is not unusual in Indian families, though sometimes it is the other way around, and the family will become the victim of the daughter-in-law. During the first few weeks, she will be very gentle and loving, but it will not take long for her real nature to emerge.

"This is what happens with people who hide their ego, just to win people over and gain control over them. They may succeed in hiding their ego for some time, but it will soon become manifest. Their real nature will be expressed of its own accord.

"A person who wears the false mask of a spiritually advanced person does not know what terrible harm he is doing. He is misleading others, and also paving the way for his own destruction. A number of sincere people may get trapped in his deception. And once they realize that they have been misled, they will lose their faith. From then on, they will be suspicious of everything that has anything to do with spirituality. They will even be suspicious of genuine masters. Think of the enormous harm that these so-called spiritual leaders are doing to society and the human race. The ego of such a person is very subtle and is difficult to get rid of. He believes that he is great. This happens naturally because he feels proud of the big crowds who attend his speeches and the praise people shower upon him. People say to him, 'Oh, you are so great and knowledgeable! What an eloquent speaker you are! You have such a presence!' With all this praise and adoration, he himself will begin to think that he is great. This thought becomes more and more ingrained in him, and as it gets deeper it also becomes subtler. He learns how to hide it and he pretends that he is great. But it won't take long for that which lies hidden within to reveal itself externally. Such people are easily fooled by others, and at times they even act foolishly."

THE BLISS-INTOXICATED MOTHER

There were clouds in the sky. It looked as if it were about to rain. The sound of the ocean waves grew louder and a strong, cool wind came blowing through the air.

Mother looked up at the sky and at once became deeply absorbed in a spiritual mood. By now the sun was completely covered by dark rain clouds. Though it was only eleven-thirty in the morning, it looked as if night were approaching. Soon it began to drizzle. Bri. Gayatri came down from Mother's room with an umbrella and held it over Mother's head. The residents didn't move but continued to sit in the rain next to Mother. Within a few seconds the rain was pouring down. But Mother continued to sit in the same spot with Her gaze still directed towards the sky.

A few minutes later Mother got up and walked into the rain, and She began to play like a child. She jumped about and danced in circles, now and then pausing in the pouring rain to look up at the sky. She would stand with Her arms outstretched, Her open palms facing up towards the sky as if She were trying to catch the rain drops in Her hands. All the residents were standing a few yards away, watching this beautiful scene.

Mother was by now completely drenched. Gayatri stood helplessly by Her side with the folded umbrella in her hands. Suddenly, Mother joined Her palms together above Her head, and began to turn around in a circle. And as She did so, She recited the following verse.

Anandam Saccitanandam
Anandam Paramanandam

Anandam Saccitanandam
Anandam Brahmanandam

The Bliss of Pure Existence/Consciousness
The Bliss of Supreme Bliss
The Bliss of Pure Existence/Consciousness
The Bliss of Absolute and Undivided Bliss ·

Long after the song had come to an end, Mother continued to circle round and round. Her palms were still joined above Her head and Her eyes were closed. There was no sign of Her having any body consciousness at all. She was transported to another world. Her face was radiant and enchanting. There was a beautiful, divine smile on Her lips, and as She continued Her dance, rain water dripped through Her black, cascading hair and streamed down Her cheeks.

Nobody knew what to do. Somebody suggested that they carry Her inside. But Br. Nealu thought that they shouldn't touch Mother as long as She was in that state of bliss. While they were discussing among themselves what to do, Mother slowly stopped Her dance and lay down on the ground, which by now had become a pool of muddy water. And as She lay in the rain without moving, the spiritual glow continued to radiate from Her face.

The rain continued to pour as heavily as before and the residents grew increasingly anxious. Bri. Gayatri who was sitting next to Mother on the soaking wet ground, trying to shield Her with the umbrella, insisted that they should carry Mother inside. Finally everyone agreed and did as she directed.

As soon as Mother had been brought into Her room, Gayatri requested everyone to leave so that she could remove Mother's wet clothes. Everybody left immediately and the door was closed. Mother remained in the state of *samadhi* for a long time.

What can one say about such a mysterious personality, who at one moment is the great Master and the next an innocent child, and who then again, a few seconds later, slips into the highest state of *samadhi*?

> *On account of constant absorption in Brahman, freed from the sense of reality of external objects, only seemingly enjoying them when offered by others, like one sleepy or like a baby, perceiving the world as something seen in a dream and recognizing it only now and then, such a man is indeed rare. He is the enjoyer of the fruits of untold merit and is truly held blessed and revered on earth.*
>
> — VIVEKACHOODAMANI

CHAPTER THIRTEEN

DIVINITY CANNOT BE BORROWED
The story of Paundra Vasudeva

*T*oday, Mother was sitting in the little room that served as a library. The question about the subtlety of the spiritual ego was raised again. One of the brahmacharins asked, "Amma, yesterday, while You were talking about the subtlety of the ego of a spiritual person, You said that sometimes such people even act like fools. How can they go to that extreme?"

Mother: "Children, why not? When people get carried away by their desire to become famous and to be admired by others they sometimes act foolishly, because when the mind becomes obsessed with something, you lose your power of discrimination. The mind loses its sense of clarity and you become an easy tool in the hands of other people. In your desire to be recognized for your greatness and for people to admire you and sing your praises, you lose your power to express yourself spontaneously and your behavior becomes unnatural. You may begin to believe that what others say about you is true, and that unless you act in a certain way, you will not be considered to be great. And so, you end up acting foolishly. When you are that mesmerized by the admiration accorded to you by others, even if somebody should happen to give you some excellent advice, it won't serve any purpose, because you will not be able to look at the truth.

"Children, do you know the story about Paundra Vasudeva, who pretended that he was Krishna? Paundra Vasudeva was the king of a country called Karurusha, at the time when Krishna reigned over Dwaraka. Paundra was too attached to his role as a king and he had an intense desire to be worshipped by his subjects. Both he and the king of Kashi were against Sri Krishna; they were jealous of Krishna's fame and the way people adored and worshipped Him. In his intense craving for fame and recognition, Paundra, with the help of the king of Kashi, finally conspired a plot against the Lord. They made a public announcement saying that the Krishna who lived in Dwaraka was a fake, and that he was not the real incarnation of Lord Vishnu. They further declared that the real Krishna, the real incarnation of Vishnu, was none other than Paundra himself.

"When people heard this they said that if their king Paundra was the real incarnation of Lord Vishnu, he should be holding the divine signs, namely the conch, discus, mace and lotus flower, in his four sacred hands. In response to this, Paundra, who by this time had

begun to believe that he really was Lord Vishnu, would
on certain occasions fix two wooden arms to his shoulders, so that he appeared to have four arms, just like
the Lord. He also made sure that he was carrying replicas
of the four sacred signs. Paundra got so carried away
that he even had a Garuda made out of wood.[12] Unfortunately, the wooden eagle couldn't fly; instead, it
was placed on top of the royal chariot. Paundra commanded his wife to dress up like the Goddess Lakshmi
and the two of them travelled around the city, blessing
people from their perch on top of the wooden Garuda.
Paundra became the laughing stock of the country.
Many people obviously thought he had gone mad.

"Those of Paundra's subjects who happened to
admire Lord Krishna were angered at this shameless,
self-aggrandizing declaration of their king, but they
didn't dare say anything against him, directly. Instead,
they mocked him by making loud comments whenever
they saw him on the streets, on top of his peculiar
chariot. They would say, 'Oh, our King really does
look like Krishna! He should wear a crown with a
peacock feather tucked in it, and he ought to be holding
a flute in his beautiful hands. And think how enchanting
it would be if his body were of a dark blue color! In fact,
he should ask for all the divine weapons that the fake
Krishna in Dwaraka is carrying. That Krishna has no

---

[12] The divine eagle, Garuda, is the *vahana* (vehicle) ridden by Lord
Vishnu.

right to those weapons. After all, they don't belong to Him. The real owner is our own king, the great Paundra Vasudeva.'

"Whenever Paundra went out, he would be met by such comments. Even the people who were close to him - the royal family and all his courtiers - began making such comments. The king got so carried away by what he heard that he painted his body blue and started dressing like Sri Krishna. He walked around in an exact replica of Krishna's costume, holding a flute in his hands, even though he had no idea how to play the flute. And he gradually came to believe that he really was Vishnu, or Krishna. Sometimes he was Vishnu and at other times he was Krishna.

"But the drama was not yet over. Considering the comments of his subjects to be a truism, he also wanted to acquire all the divine weapons of Sri Krishna. He consequently sent a messenger to Dwaraka saying, 'Cowherd, You are nothing but a fake. Hand over all the divine weapons, including the divine discus, which rightfully belong to me - the real Krishna, the true incarnation of Lord Vishnu - or be prepared to die in the battlefield.'

"When Krishna received the message He said, 'Very well. But I would like to hand the weapons over in person. Ask Paundra to come and receive them.' Sri Krishna wanted to teach the foolhardy king a good lesson.

"Paundra arrived at the prearranged meeting place, along with his entire army, prepared to fight if necessary. He was dressed in the costume of Lord Vishnu. When Paundra and his army arrived, Sri Krishna was already waiting for him. As soon as Paundra saw Krishna, he shouted at the top of his voice, 'You fake! Don't try to play Your tricks on me! Surrender the divine weapons and the discus, or be prepared to die!' In the battle which followed, Sri Krishna destroyed Paundra's entire army. When it was all over, Sri Krishna stood holding the divine discus with His index finger. With a mischievous smile on His face, He said, 'Paundra, I have come for no other reason than to give you this weapon. Here it comes! Take it, it's yours!' With these words, Krishna released the divine discus from His finger. You can imagine what happened. The discus sliced through Paundra's neck and he fell dead to the ground. Thus the king's foolish attachment to fame and self-glorification was destroyed by Lord Krishna, the Perfect Master, and he was released from the self-created ego."

Question: "Does this mean that only a Perfect Master, who is beyond the mind and the ego, can save a person from the grip of the subtle ego?"

Mother: "That is right. An extremely powerful weapon like the divine discus is needed to pierce the subtle ego. But this weapon is under the sole control of the Perfect Master. It is the weapon of true knowledge, the weapon of the Master's omniscience, omnipotence and all-pervasiveness.

"A person who has a mad craving for fame, and for power and prestige, will want to grab everything in the world. He will become so foolish that he might even declare, 'I am the greatest and therefore I have a right to everything.' He will lose all his power of discrimination and will be completely clouded by his thoughts of power and self-glorification.

"People who have been blinded in this way are likely to forget God. In their mad pursuit to gain the respect and admiration of others, they sometimes challenge God. But when they do this, it also means that they are about to be exposed.

"Divinity cannot be borrowed or imitated. Divine love and other divine qualities cannot be imitated.

CHAPTER FOURTEEN

*T*his night was a great festive occasion. It was *Tiruvatira*, a special festival which is celebrated all over Kerala. In India, Lord Shiva and the Goddess Parvati are considered to be the Universal Father and Mother. On the day of Tiruvatira, the married women of Kerala take a vow of fasting during which they pray for the well being of their husbands. It is also part of the tradition that they should stay awake that night, praying and singing to the glory of Shiva and Parvati.

A group of elderly women from the village and some women who were staying at the Ashram were standing in a circle, in the front yard of the temple. They were about to begin the celebration with the *Tiruvatirakali,* an ancient, traditional folk dance performed by the women of Kerala.

All the ashramites were sitting in front of the temple. Mother was sitting under the mailanchy tree, surrounded by a dozen children. Some of them were from the neighborhood, others were the children of devotees. Mother was in a playful mood; one could hear the sound of laughter and loud conversation coming from Her direction. Everyone was more interested in what Mother was doing, than in watching the dance. But even though all eyes were fixed on Her, everyone stayed

instinctively at a distance, not wanting to go near and
so disturb the beautiful picture of Mother and the children.

The older women now began the traditional singing and dancing. They sang *Thirukathakal Padam...*

> *O Goddess Durga*
> *O Kali*
> *remove my bad fate*
> *Each day I beg to receive a vision*
> *of Your form.*
>
> *Let me sing in praise of Your sacred acts*
> *Please give me a boon*
> *and when I sing of Your glories*
> *please come into my heart.*
>
> *O Essence of the Vedas*
> *I do not know the methods of meditation,*
> *and my music lacks a melody.*
> *Have mercy on me*
> *Let me immerse myself in bliss.*
>
> *You are Gayatri,*
> *You are fame and Liberation,*
> *Kartyayani, Haimavati, and Kakshayani*[13]
> *You are the very soul of Realization*
> *my sole refuge.*

---

[13] Names of Devi

O Devi
give me the power to speak
on the essential ideas.
I understand that without You,
the embodiment of the Universe,
Shiva, the Causative Principle,
would exist no more.

THIS IS 'THAT'

The song reached a very high tempo. At this point
Mother got up from the place where She had been
sitting with the children and went over to the women
who were dancing. She looked very excited and at the
same time divinely intoxicated as She joined in the
dance. There was an innocent expression on Her face
which made Her look like a divine child among the
dancing women. The women were overjoyed to have
Mother dancing in their midst.

At one stage of the dance, two ladies facing each
other made a pair and clapped their open palms together.
Mother who was transported to another world was still
dancing but in Her own blissful way. Her eyes were closed
and both hands were held in divine *mudras*. After dancing
in circles with the ladies for some time, Mother moved
towards the center of the dance where She continued
to dance blissfully, while the devotees were singing a
song, glorifying the Goddess Parvati.

After some time Mother stopped dancing and came

to a standstill. Her external form and Her countenance were radiating with a divine glow. She looked exactly as She did during Devi Bhava. It was evident that She was still absorbed in Her divine mood. The devotees continued to dance and to sing, one song after another, until Mother finally sat down on the ground, still in that indrawn state.

The devotees had a strong feeling that Mother was in the bhava of the Goddess Parvati. Who knows? Perhaps She was revealing that mood for the benefit of the devotees. Nothing is impossible for a soul who is one with the Supreme Brahman. Such a person can manifest any aspect of the Divine at any time he wants.

When Mother finally returned to Her normal self, one of the devotees asked Her, "Amma, we strongly felt that You were in the divine mood of Goddess Parvati?" Mother pointed first at Herself and then upward, as She replied, "This is That." After a pause She continued, "Whether or not it is manifested, this is That. Don't mistake this for the body. The body is only a cover. There is infinity beyond the cover."

The incomprehensible expression on Mother's face and the words that She uttered seemed to be coming directly from the highest plane of consciousness. If one penetrated a little, it was not difficult to discern that Mother, though not directly, was saying that She was in the divine mood of the Goddess Parvati. The depth of such a declaration was so profound and piercing that everyone was deeply touched in the innermost recesses of their hearts.

THE IMPORTANCE OF
FEMININE QUALITIES IN A SEEKER

A few minutes passed in silence until one visiting devotee was unable to resist the temptation to ask a question. "Amma, I have heard of two kinds of disciples: those who are predominantly intellectual and those who are more feminine in nature. I don't think that I have understood this properly. Could you kindly enlighten me on this point?

Mother: Spiritual realization cannot be attained without love, devotion and an openness which allows one to receive true knowledge from a real Master. A seeker who is predominantly intellectual in nature must therefore try to create a balance between the intellect and the heart. He must have immense love for his Master and at the same time he should have a proper knowledge about his Master's omniscient nature.

If you are too intellectual, it could create an imbalance and you will become too egoistic. Intellect is reasoning. It can only dissect and cut asunder. It cannot unite. It won't help faith and love to develop, which is an essential factor for a spiritual seeker's inner growth. Too much intellect is not good for a seeker, because he will lack love and devotion towards his Master. Without love and an attitude of self-surrender and humility, the Master cannot impart true knowledge to you.

"It would be difficult to discipline a seeker who is predominantly intellectual, unless an all-powerful Master takes charge of him. Only a perfect Master can break his ego and bring out the real essence that is his true nature. He may then outwardly retain his intellectual qualities, but within he will be deeply devotional; there will be a perfect balance between the two qualities.

"When the Master has worked on the ego, the ego becomes useful to the world. His characteristics will be refined and well moulded, and by the Master's Grace, his ego will be well under control.

"When the ego, through the Master's Grace, is perfectly under control, the disciple does everything in the Master's name. The Master does everything through him, and he himself has no place in what he does. His attitude will be, 'I am only an instrument. My all-powerful Master does everything through me.' He attributes everything to the Master and will take no credit for anything. But at the same time, he will have an adventurous mind, tremendous courage and the power to undertake seemingly impossible tasks and drive them to the goal.

"But this chiselling, moulding and rebuilding of the disciple's ego can only be done by a Satguru. If such a seeker is on his own or if he is being trained by an imperfect guru, it will only create a further imbalance in his nature, in some way or other. This in turn will do a lot of harm to others and to society as a whole. He will soon try to become a guru himself. You may see him trying to form his own group of disciples and building his own ashram.

"In Hanuman, the great devotee of Lord Rama, one can find a beautiful blending of both masculine and feminine qualities. He did everything in the name of Rama, his beloved Lord, and he took no credit for anything. Even though Hanuman succeeded in doing very difficult tasks, he was never proud of any of his feats. On the contrary, he remained the humble and obedient servant of his Master, Lord Rama. 'Not by my power and strength, but by Lord Rama's Grace,' was always Hanuman's attitude.

Disciples with feminine qualities are entirely different. They do not want to go out and preach, nor do they want any attention or respect. They do not even worry about attaining Self-Realization. Their only wish is to stay in the Master's physical presence and to serve him. That is their *tapas*. They know of no spirituality higher than that. For them, there is no higher Truth than their Master. 'My Master, my World, my All in all,' is their attitude. Such a disciple's heart is full of love and attachment towards his Master. This relationship cannot be explained through logic or reasoning. It can only be compared to the love of the *gopis* towards Krishna: Love, love, love and love. Overflowing love. That's it. They don't care about anything else."

Mother then shared a story about one of Buddha's disciples.

"One day a certain disciple suddenly disappeared. Nobody could find him anywhere. Seven days passed, but still nobody knew where he was. Then one day, Buddha found him lying on the roof of the ashram. Buddha knew that he was there and knew that the disciple had attained enlightenment. Buddha held his hand and said, 'I know that you have attained the state of *nirvana.*'

"The disciple said, 'My beloved Master, I know that it has happened, I don't need any confirmation from You. In fact, I am afraid of Your confirmation, because the next thing You say to me will be, 'Now that you have attained *nirvana*, you must go out and preach, you must spread the message of Truth throughout the world.' I am afraid, my Lord, because I would much rather have to stay in Your presence remaining in a state of ignorance, than have to leave You and go out into the world fully realized.' "

"This is the attitude of a disciple who is endowed with feminine qualities. He will always remain deeply in love with his Master. The heart of a feminine disciple is so full of love for the Master that he always wants to remain in the Master's physical presence. That is the fulfillment of his life. That is his highest realization."

A TRUE MASTER IS
THE UNIVERSE AND BEYOND

Question: "Amma, I have heard you say that bowing down in utter humility to the Master is equal to bowing down to all of existence. Please tell us what You mean by that?"

Mother: "Children, only when you become completely egoless can you bow down to all of creation. When there is no ego, you go beyond the limitations of the mind and become the all-pervasive Self. Once you behold everything as your own Self, you can only bow down and accept. When you go beyond the ego, it means that you become nothing. But, like space you become everything, you become all of creation.

"Once, when Krishna was a child, He was playing with His friends. They were playing with all sorts of imaginary things, just as small children will do, and they were having great fun. Krishna was going to eat with His friends. One of the children served a meal of sand to everyone, imagining that it was rice. They were supposed to only pretend that they were eating, but Krishna actually ate the sand. Krishna's older brother, Balaram, and the others immediately ran and told Yashoda, the Lord's foster mother, what had happened. Yashoda seized Krishna and asked Him to open His mouth. Lo and behold! She saw the entire universe inside His mouth. She saw the sun, the moon and the stars, the Milky Way and all the galaxies. She saw mountains, valleys, forests, trees and animals. Yashoda beheld the entire universe within Krishna.

"In a similar manner, during the battle at Kurukshetra, while Krishna was giving Arjuna the great sermon of the Bhagavad Gita, the Lord showed His universal form to Arjuna, when he expressed a desire to see it. Arjuna then also saw the whole universe within the Lord's form. He even saw the Pandava and Kaurava forces on the Lord's body.

"What does this mean? It means that the entire universe is contained within the true Master. Krishna was a true Master, and a true Master is God. His consciousness is one with the Universal Consciousness. That Consciousness is one and the same Consciousness that shines in and through all of creation. Such a great Master has an infinite number of bodies, an infinite number of eyes. He sees, hears, smells, eats, and breathes through every body. He is infinity itself. Surrendering to such a Master with complete humility is the same thing as surrendering to all of existence, and bowing down to the whole of creation.

"In that state you realize that nothing is different or separate from you. Bowing down to all of existence is also a state of total acceptance. You stop fighting with the situations that arise in your life. You fight and struggle only when you have an ego, only when you are identified with the body. When you shake off the shackles of the ego, no more fighting is possible. You can only accept.

"While an egotistic person considers everyone except himself to be an ignorant fool, a true *Mahatma* beholds everyone as an extension of his own Self. In the state of Self-Realization one cannot reject anything - one can only accept. Space accepts everything, whether good or bad. A river accepts everything, and the ocean accepts everything. You can accommodate anything and everything when you become as vast as the universe. When your mind and ego disappear, you become infinity.

"Space and Nature accept the polluted air from factories as well as the sweet fragrance of flowers. They embrace everything. Likewise, a true *Mahatma* welcomes everything, both negative and positive. He accepts everyone, and out of his unconditional love and infinite compassion he gives only grace and blessings in return.

"Children, have you heard this story? An unmarried village girl once gave birth to a child. At first she refused to tell anyone who the father was, but after repeated questioning she finally named a highly respected spiritual Master, who lived at the outskirts of the village. The girl's parents, followed by the villagers, stormed into the Master's house. They insulted him, they beat him up and accused him of being a hypocrite. They brought the baby to him and ordered him to take care of it. The Master took the baby in his arms, looked at it lovingly and said, 'Very well. So be it.' From then on, the *Mahatma* looked after the baby with great care. He treated it with as much love and tenderness as a mother towards her own child. The Master's reputation was ruined. He was shunned by all the villagers and by his own disciples. Yet, even after everyone had abandoned him, the Master said calmly, 'Very well. So be it.' A year passed by. The girl who had given birth to the child was being troubled by a guilty conscience, and finally confessed that the father of the child was the young man next door and not the innocent saint. Her parents, the villagers and the disciples were filled with remorse. They all went to see the *Mahatma* and fell at his feet, asking him to forgive them. And they asked him to return the child. The unperturbed *Mahatma* smiled as he handed them the child. He blessed everyone and once again said calmly, 'Very well. So be it.'

"This is the attitude of a true *Mahatma*. He bows down to existence. It is not his nature to reject anything. He does not say no to life or any of life's experiences. He simply says yes to everything that life brings him. He does not curse or take revenge; he only forgives and blesses.

"With the exception of human beings, all of creation stands as an example of thankfulness to the Creator for the infinite blessings He showers upon it. Even birds and animals live their lives in gratitude. Nothing errs from its own nature, whether it be of the plant or animal kingdom. Everything lives according to the laws of nature. But so-called intelligent human beings are breaking the laws and disturbing the harmony of nature. They disturb the life of other living beings and other aspects of creation.

"God has blessed man with an abundance of gifts, but man turns everything into a curse. This life is a wonderful blessing. Our mind and every limb of our body, our health and our riches - all are blessings bestowed on us by God. But what are we doing with these blessings? We use our hands to do wrong actions, our legs carry us to prohibited places, we use our eyes to look at ugly things, with our minds we make unrighteous plans and think ill of others, we use our intellect to invent destructive things, and whatever wealth we have, we use it only for our own selfish purposes. We have made life a curse for ourselves and for others.

"All creatures once approached Lord Brahma, the Creator. They all had an intense desire to escape from the sorrow and suffering of life. The pig stepped forward first. With tears rolling down his cheeks he pleaded with the Lord, "Oh Lord of all creation, is there any escape from this suffering? Is there any hope for my species?" The creator nodded positively and said, "Yes, my child. Of course." Next came the bullock, the dog and the elephant. They all cried and asked the same question. And to all of them, the Creator said, 'There is hope for every one of you.' Then, man stepped forward with the same request. Lord Brahma looked at man, and suddenly the Creator Himself burst into tears." An uproarious laughter followed. When it had quietened down, Mother said, "Today is Tiruvatira. We are supposed to sing in praise of Shiva and Parvati. So, let us now sing and dance. Mother then spontaneously started to sing a song in the exalted mood of supreme devotion. Everybody responded to Mother's singing with great love and enthusiasm. The song, *Indukaladhara*, glorifies Lord Shiva and the Goddess Parvati. Mother sang the refrain repeatedly in a very high tempo.

Shambho Shankara Shambho Shankara
Shambho Shankara Shiva Shambho

O Lord Shiva
who carries the crescent moon
on His head
who keeps the Holy Ganges
in His matted hair locks
whose body is adorned with serpents
and whose fragrance is Divine
I prostrate
at the Holy Feet
of that Supreme Lord.

O Lord
who is the Primordial Cause
who is extremely compassionate
towards His devotees
The great God

who bestows auspicious boons
who holds the trident
and whose Feet are being worshipped
also by celestial beings
O Destroyer of all afflictions
Shambho Shankara.....

O Lord of the Universe
I take refuge at Your feet
O Lord, Beloved of Parvati
O compassionate One
Remove my endless sorrows
and give me refuge
at Your Feet.

Everyone seemed to be in ecstasy. At one point Mother got up and began to dance, and everybody else also got up.

The devotees clapped their hands and sang loudly, forming a perfect circle around Mother. As they sang the words, *Shambho Shankara Shambho Shankara...,* they moved slowly and rhythmically around Mother. Mother remained in the middle of the circle dancing in supreme bliss.

Living with a great Master is an indescribable experience. It is like a constant festival, and each moment is a celebration. The word festival in Sanskrit is *utsavam.* The original word is *utsravam*, which means to rise up and flow, or to overflow. All festivals are symbolic of the overflowing of pure bliss and consciousness; especially the festivals that are celebrated in temples symbolize the overflow of spiritual energy and bliss.

The spiritual energy that is created in the temple through prayer, meditation, worship and chanting, fills the temple compound. It then rises above the four walls of the temple and overflows into the entire village or city where it is situated, purifying the whole environment. This is the idea behind the festivals that are celebrated in the temples every year.

In Mother's presence it happens unceasingly, for Her presence is a never-ending stream of divine energy, which overflows from Her being into the hearts of Her devotees. They experience that divine energy as they drink it in. This is what was happening now and what is happening always.

The dancing and singing continued, until Mother suddenly broke out of the circle and walked away toward the southern end of the Ashram, to the edge of the backwaters. The women immediately stopped dancing as if an electric switch had been turned off. Everybody turned to see what Mother was about to do, but nobody followed Her, because She gave the impression of wanting to be alone. One of the senior brahmacharins asked everyone to go and meditate. Within a few minutes they all dispersed and the whole night was spent in meditation and prayer.

CHAPTER FIFTEEN

IS ATTACHMENT TO THE
SATGURU'S FORM IMPORTANT?

*M*other was answering a question asked by one of the Western devotees.

Question: "Amma, some people are very attached to Your external form. They have so much love for You that they have an intense craving to be in Your physical presence. Whereas, there are others who do not have that kind of attachment, although they truly long to realize God. They love You, but they are of the opinion that being attached to Your form will cause pain, and because of this, they stay away. Amma, I am wondering if it's absolutely necessary to be attached to the Master's physical form, or is it sufficient to have the longing to realize God, without being attached to the external form?"

Mother: "The most important trait that a true *sadhak* should have is the attitude of complete self-surrender and acceptance. In the beginning stages of spirituality, it is hard to surrender and accept everything, especially if there is no one there to guide you, someone who you can look upon as an example. One should have at least the willingness to surrender. But confusion can always arise as to whom or what one is supposed to surrender. How is it done? Until you have attained Self-Realization, you can only have a vague idea about all the aspects of spirituality. Your unsteady, suspicious mind will always raise doubts. If there is no one there to guide you, you will be confused and easily misled, and you don't know who to turn to. So to begin with, the need for a true Master arises; someone you can relate to and learn true surrender and acceptance from. Surrender and acceptance is not something that you are simply taught. You can not learn it by studying books, or from a school or university. It will develop within you from the tremendous inspiration you receive through the Master's physical presence, for the Master is the embodiment of all divine qualities. In the Master, you observe true surrender and acceptance, and thus you are given a real example that you can relate to, something tangible to commit yourself to. The immensely inspiring and transforming presence of the Master creates a deep love within you towards the Master, and a strong bond develops between you. Surrender and acceptance are usually born when pure love arises within.

JUST LIKE A CARING MOTHER

"In the primary stages of spiritual love there is the

attitude that, 'I am Your devotee, disciple, servant, or lover, and You are my Lord, Master, or Beloved.' In this initial period, you have fallen in love with the Master and thus cannot go beyond the form. You are so attached to the external form of the Master, that you don't want to go beyond it. Since this is the primary stage, you are slowly learning surrender and acceptance, but it is not yet complete. Spiritually, you are just a newborn baby, for you know nothing about the world of spirituality. Just as a baby drinks nothing but its mother's breast milk and knows of nothing but the warmth of her bosom, the spiritual baby in you knows only about the form and the physical closeness of your Master. As far as you are concerned, the Master's external form is the whole world of spirituality, and you become extremely attached to it. You need the physical presence and the warmth of your Master, and you will always crave it.

"Just as crying is the only manner of expression a child uses to let its wishes be known - be it hunger, thirst or pain - in the beginning stages of spirituality you have only one way of expressing your heart, and that is through shedding tears of intense longing. The Master will bind you with his love and he will become the absolute center of your life. In that experience of divine, unconditional love you have nothing to say. You will just silently shed tears of love and longing.

"As a spiritual baby, you are born into a totally

strange and unknown world. A baby needs warmth and its mother's milk. The mother knows the heart of her child and will do everything for him. Her breasts spontaneously fill with milk for the baby, whenever he is hungry. The mother intuitively knows if her baby is in any pain or discomfort. If the baby is lying in urine or excreta, the mother will come and bathe the child and change his clothes. The baby falls asleep listening to the sound of its mother's voice as she sings it a beautiful lullaby. Thus, the baby cannot live without its mother. A mother or a motherly person is absolutely necessary for a child's healthy growth. A real mother nourishes not only the child's body but also its mind. The child's world revolves around its mother. He is completely dependent on her. To him his mother is the most beautiful being in the whole world. Because he is so attached to her, all his dreams and fantasies are woven around her.

"In a similar way, the spiritual Master is everything to the *sadhak* at the beginning of his spiritual life. It can never be an exaggeration then to state that the Master is everything to a true disciple, even more than God.

"As a mother is the whole world to her baby, a true Master is everything to the disciple who is just a beginner, a baby on the spiritual path. And the Master has even more concern for his spiritual baby than a mother for her newborn babe.

"In the beginning stages of spirituality the disciple

assumes the role of a child towards the Master. For the disciple the whole of spirituality can be put in a nutshell: 'My Master, my All in all.' All his imagination and all his dreams about spirituality are woven around the Master. The disciple is extremely attached to his Master, always wanting his love and affection, his attention and his warmth, wanting always to remain in his physical presence. He cannot dream of a world or a life without his Master. This is a very spontaneous and natural feeling on the part of the devotee or disciple.

"But the baby never remains a baby, for he grows under the loving care of his mother. Likewise, the spiritual baby grows under the guidance of the Master, but his growth is internal. As the spiritual child grows, the mother in the Master slowly changes into the father, and the disciplinarian in the Master is invoked. This disciplining is meant to teach the disciple detachment, self-surrender and acceptance, not only to the external form of the Master, but towards all of creation. The Master is not just the body - he is the power that shines in and through everything, and therefore he teaches the disciple to bow down in humility before all of creation. This training serves to lift the disciple from narrowmindedness to a higher level, allowing him to experience everything in a broader way. He will then realize that everything in existence is nothing but his own Master. Through the Master's training it will be impressed upon the disciple that the Master is not just the physical human form, but the one Consciousness that pervades all of creation. As the disciple grows internally and matures, the Master lets him become more and more independent, that is, dependent on his own Self.

"In the final stage of love, the lover and the Beloved become one. Even beyond this, there comes a state where there is no love, lover or Beloved. That state is beyond expression. That is where the Master finally takes you.

"The way of a true Master is far beyond words. Unlike the mother in the world, a true Master never binds the disciple to him. On the contrary, he takes the disciple beyond all limitations and attachments of the body and makes him completely independent and free. Attachment to the Master's body will eventually take you to complete detachment and freedom. Even though the disciple will feel a strong attachment towards the Master's external form in the early stages of his development, you cannot call it bondage. Two people who dwell on the physical plane can bind each other, but a true Master cannot bind anyone, for the Master is not the body. He is not personal in the way we think of our personal friends or other people. The Master is both impersonal and personal. Bondage exists if you are attached only to the person's body. When you love the Master's external form you are not loving a limited individual, you are loving Pure Consciousness, and the Master will slowly reveal this to you. As your

awareness grows internally, that is, as your awareness
of the Master's true nature deepens, you will gradually
experience the Master's all-pervasive nature. You will
come to know that the Master is not limited to the
body, that he is the *Atma Shakti* immanent in everything. The Master himself will take you through this
experience. His Grace will finally help you go beyond
all bondage. That is why Amma says that your attachment to the Master's external form can never bind you."

A TRUE MASTER DESTROYS ALL PAIN

Question: "Is Amma saying that attachment to the Master's
external form is necessary? But what about all the pain
that some people are talking about - the pain connected
to one's attachment to the Master?"

Mother: "Amma doesn't understand the strange concepts people have. You are saying that because there is
some pain involved if one is attached to the Master's
form, one does not want to be attached to it. Children,
can you point somebody out to Amma who is not in pain
in this world? People are constantly in pain, either physically
or mentally. Ask anyone in the world and they will tell you,
'My body is suffering so much,' or 'My feelings are hurt,'
or 'So and so didn't treat me with respect and I feel
insulted.' Tell Amma who is not in pain! People are
undergoing pain either internally or externally. What
do you know about pain? Pain does not involve just

physical pain. The inner wounds are much more painful. There is no logic in you saying that attachment to the Master's external form will create pain. You are carrying deep wounds within you that have been caused by the past. All those wounds and the pain that comes from them are the result of your over attachment to the pleasures of the world. You are not bothered about your pus infected wounds and the pain they cause. All those wounds remain unhealed. Nobody can heal them, because you are carrying the wounds and tendencies from your previous lives. They are not just from this lifetime. No doctor or psychotherapist can heal those wounds. They cannot penetrate that deep into your mind and remove your wounds. Your wounds and tendencies lie deep within you; they are very old and have slowly started gnawing you from inside.

"People turn to experts to lessen their inner pain, but all the experts in the world, the doctors, scientists, psychologists etc., are people who dwell in their own minds, within the small world created by their egos. As long as they themselves have not penetrated into their own minds, how can they penetrate into others? As long as they themselves are in the grip of their mind and ego, how can they help others to go beyond the mind and ego? They too have deep wounds and strong tendencies, just like you. Such experts cannot help you to heal your wounds and remove the pain. Only a true Master, who is completely free from such limitations and who is beyond the mind, can penetrate into your mind and treat all those unhealed wounds and remove all your strong tendencies and old habits.

"It is very strange to hear you say that there are those who do not want to be attached to the Master's form because there is pain involved. You are already experiencing a tremendous amount of pain. In fact, you are the very embodiment of deep, agonizing pain. Attachment to the Master's form cannot create any pain whatsoever, because he is not an object, nor is he a body or an ego. He is beyond. He cannot possibly hurt you, or enforce anything upon you. He is like space, like the boundless sky, and space cannot hurt you. So, do not project your preconceived ideas onto the Master, or try to judge him. The mind is inherently wrong; it is incapable of making any sound judgement. All your concepts and your judgement belong to your mind and have nothing to do with the perfect Master who is beyond the mind. A mind can perhaps judge another mind, but the mind cannot judge that which is beyond itself. A mind or ego can hurt another mind or ego, but someone who is beyond the mind cannot hurt anybody, because such a soul has no ego or judgement to direct towards anybody. Your pain lies within yourself, it does not come from the Master.

"When you are in the physical presence of a great Master, a *Satguru*, you are made to look at all your pain. It has been lying hidden within you and it now becomes manifest, because a true Master is like the sun, a spiritual sun. There is no night in his presence. There is constant daylight. When the sun of the Master shines, it penetrates deep into your mind, and in its light you see everything within you. You see the hidden hell that lies within you, and now that you have seen it, you know that it is there. It has always been there, but you never knew it. How can you remove your hidden pain if you are not aware of its presence? It is important to know that the pain is coming from within you, and not from somewhere outside. Until now you have thought that the pain came from external factors; from broken relationships, from unfulfilled desires, from someone's death, or from the anger of others, their insults and abuse. But the real source of that pain is to be found within you. And now, in the light of the Master's infinite spiritual glory, you are made to see everything clearly. You realize that all the pain exists within you.

"Remember that the Master is not simply going to leave you there all alone. He will help you by using his infinite spiritual energy. He will heal your wounds.

"So, the pain does not stem from your attachment to the Master's external form, it is your mind and your negative tendencies that create the pain. When you come to understand the nature of your pain, you need to cooperate with the Master. He is the divine doctor, whose capacity and energy is inexhaustible.

"Remember that you are a patient in need of major surgery. But don't worry, you can trust this doctor completely. Have undivided faith in him. You are in his operation room. Let him work on you; cooperate with him and don't struggle; be still and do not move. Of course, he will give you anesthesia. His anesthesia is the unconditional love and compassion that he expresses through his entire being, and with that anesthesia you will be made ready for the operation.

"Once the Master begins to operate he is not going to let you go, because no doctor will let his patient run away when the operation is only half over. In one way or another, the Master will see that you remain on the operation table, because it would be dangerous if you were to run away in the middle of the procedure. The Satguru won't let you run away. But the surgery performed by the Satguru is not very painful, compared to the worst condition of your disease, and in relation to the highest bliss and the other benefits that you will gain. The Master's overflowing love and compassion will greatly lessen the pain. The true Master is one with God, and therefore, you will be basking in God's love and compassion.

"The Master is not a pain giver, he is a pain killer. His intention is not to give you temporary relief, but permanent relief - forever. But for some reason people want to keep their pain. Even though supreme bliss is our nature, it seems that in their present mental state, people enjoy their pain, as if it has become a natural part of them.

"A palm reader was reading someone's hand and he predicted, 'Until the age of fifty you will experience a lot of sorrow and suffering in your life. You will be in constant mental pain and agony.' 'And after the age of fifty?' asked the customer. The palm reader said coolly, 'After the age of fifty it will become your nature.'

There was tremendous laughter and even Mother joined in. She continued, "It seems that human nature has almost become like this. People are in pain, and they have almost become identified with it. So much so, that they are not even aware of it, nor do they really want to get out of it."

The brahmacharin who had asked the question said, "Amma, I still have one more question." He looked at Mother to see Her reaction, because sometimes Mother remains quiet without responding to any questions. Mother's ways are always puzzling and unpredictable. Nobody knows when She will choose to speak or not. Even in the midst of a brainstorming discussion Mother will suddenly slip into Her own infinite consciousness. Her endless moods are beyond human understanding. It can happen anywhere and at any time.

NONE OTHER THAN
THE SUPREME GODDESS

Once, some devotees wanted to take Mother to a
famous Devi temple in Tamil Nadu. This incident
happened in the middle of 1977. During this period
Mother would frequently become completely oblivious
to all outer circumstances. At such times She didn't
have the least awareness of Her body.

The family who wished to take Mother to the temple
were very devoted to Her. In those days it wasn't as
crowded around Mother as it is today. The devotees
would come only during the Bhava *darshan*, and the
following morning, when it was over, they often invited Mother to their homes. Mother would sometimes
go and spend a day or two with them. The devotees
hoped that if She came to their home, they could look
after Her for a day or two and She would be able to get
some rest. In those days, Mother never ate or slept unless
somebody was there to remind Her, and, if need be,
pester Mother and insist that She should rest and eat
something, at least now and then. But even so, it was
very difficult. She never bothered about Her bodily needs.
Most of the time, Mother remained in a totally absorbed mood.

The Krishna and Devi Bhavas were manifested three
nights a week (Tuesdays, Thursdays and Sundays).
On all these days Mother would spend twelve to thir-

teen hours receiving people. On Bhava *darshan* days, the evening *bhajan* started at three-thirty or four p.m. and lasted until six p.m. During the first half of the night there was Krishna Bhava, which usually began at six-thirty, and during the second half there was Devi Bhava. Suppose there were two thousand people there - all of the two thousand would go up to Her twice - first to Krishna and then to Devi. The Devi Bhava sometimes ended at seven or eight in the morning.

In those days only a few families were really close to Mother; that is, only a few families had the good fortune to understand that Mother was abiding in the highest state of spiritual realization. This particular family who invited Mother to the famous Devi temple was one such family. At first Mother didn't show any interest in going, but as always, She finally yielded to their innocent prayers.

On the subject of temples, Mother once said, "The outer temple is for those who have not realized the constant presence of God within their own heart. Once that realization takes place, God's presence pervades everything, both within and without. For such a person, every place, every inch of this universe becomes a temple."

The following is a story which Mother tells to illustrate this point.

"Namdev was a highly evolved devotee of Lord Krishna. He was instructed by the Lord Himself to go and surrender to a certain enlightened soul (Vishobukechara) who was staying in a Shiva temple at the outskirts of a village. Having reached the temple, the devotee saw an old man lying down in the inner sanctum, with his feet resting on the *Shiva Lingam*. Infuriated at the sight of such sacrilege Namdev clapped his hands loudly to wake up the old man. The old man heard the noise and opened his eyes. He looked at the newcomer and said, 'Oh yes! You are Namdev who Vittal[14] sent, aren't you?' The devotee was wonderstruck and knew that he was standing before a great soul. But still, there was one thing he couldn't understand, and he said to the old man, 'You are undoubtedly a great being, but I don't understand how you can rest your feet on the Lingam?' 'Oh, are they on the Lingam? I didn't know that. Kindly remove them for me. I am too tired,' said the saint. Namdev lifted the old mans legs away from the Lingam and placed them on the floor, but amazingly, wherever he put them, a Shiva Lingam appeared. Namdev moved the saint's feet to different places, but always a Shiva Lingam would appear at the exact spot where the feet would touch. Finally, Namdev placed them on his own lap, and as he did so, he himself attained the state of Shiva.

"A true *Mahatma* is God, Himself. He doesn't need to go to any temple or place of worship, because the place where he dwells is a temple in itself. But sometimes he visits sacred places just to set an example."

---

[14] An aspect of Lord Krishna

However, Mother visited the temple to make the devotees happy. When they arrived at the temple, they walked up and stood in front of the entrance, from where one could clearly see the image of Devi, the Divine Mother, through the open doorway which led into the inner sanctum. When Mother saw the image of Devi She immediately went into a state of *samadhi*, and She remained standing absolutely still for more than one and a half hours. The members of the family were very frightened by this. Mother remained where She was, immovable as a mountain. What greatly surprised them was the posture in which She stood. Mother was standing in exactly the same pose as the Divine Mother inside the sanctum.

The family was wondering how to bring Mother back to Her normal, external consciousness, when a middle aged woman suddenly approached them. There was a dignified look on her face, but she also seemed deeply devoted and sincere. In a commanding tone she addressed the head of the family, "Can't you see that that one (pointing at Devi inside the inner sanctum) and this one (pointing at Mother who was in deep *samadhi*) are one and the same? Chant the *Meenakshi Stotram!*" The authenticity of the lady's words were such that the head of the family, like an obedient child, spontaneously began chanting the ancient Sanskrit hymn to the Divine Mother.

O Sri Vidya
who adorns the left side of Shiva,[15]
the One who is worshipped by the King of kings,
who is the embodiment of all gurus
beginning with Lord Vishnu,
Treasure Chest of Chintamani,
wish-bestowing Divine Gem,
the One, whose Feet are worshipped by the Goddess
Saraswati
and the Goddess Girija,
Consort of Shambho, the Sweet Heart of Shiva,
who is dazzling like the midday sun,
the daughter of King Malayadwaja,
Save me, O Mother Meenakshi.

While he chanted the Stotram, the woman herself remained in a deeply prayerful mood, with her eyes closed and palms joined together.

After a few minutes Mother returned to Her normal mood, but She continued standing in the same spot, swaying slightly sidewards. Her gaze was still fixed on the statue of Devi, or somewhere; it was impossible to say where exactly. The family then finally stopped chanting.

The unknown woman who had told the family to sing the *Meenakshi Stotram,* fell at Mother's feet and remained there for a long time, until Mother bent down and lovingly pulled her up towards Her. There was an extraordinary expression of love on Mother's countenance as

---

[15] i.e., who is the Consort of Shiva

She looked at the woman's face. The woman seemed to be in a state of bliss. Mother continued to look at her for a long time. Finally, She gently drew the woman's head onto Her shoulder. The woman was shedding tears of bliss as she rested on Mother's shoulder. Nobody knew who the woman was or where she had come from.

This is just one among countless such incidents which have happened around Mother. The woman who had come to the temple at that moment was like a divine messenger who wanted to remind everyone, especially the family, that Mother is the Supreme Goddess Herself.

This is why the brahmacharin who wanted to ask another question suddenly stopped and looked at Mother. He wanted to make sure that Mother was in Her normal mood. When he saw that Mother was willing to answer his question he continued.

ATTACHMENT TO A SATGURU
IS ATTACHMENT TO GOD

Question: "Amma, I am still wondering whether this attachment to the Master's external form is necessary, or if mere longing to realize God is sufficient to reach the ultimate goal?"

Mother: "Children, first of all remember that an attachment to the Master is an attachment to God. Your problem is that you try to differentiate between God and the true Master. Attachment to a true Master's physical form intensifies your longing to realize the Supreme. It is like living with God. He makes your spiritual journey much easier. Such a Master is both the means and the end. But at the same time there must be a conscious effort to see the Master in all of creation. One must also try one's best to obey the Master's words and adhere to his instructions.

"Do you have any idea about God or the supreme state of realization? You have heard about it and read about it, that's all. Whatever you have heard and read were only words. But the experience is something far beyond. It is an incomprehensible mystery.

"You cannot experience the state of God-consciousness through your mere senses or through the scriptures that you have learned. To experience it, you need to develop a new eye, the inner, or third eye. The two eyes that you have now should become one, only then can you see God. This means that even while you are seeing everything with both your eyes, you should not see the dual world. All duality disappears and you behold the oneness of creation, the whole universe. The inner eye, or the eye of true knowledge, can only be opened by a real Master."

This statement of Mother's reminds one of a famous saying of Sri Krishna, the Perfect Master, to his disciple, Arjuna:

"You cannot have an experience of Me merely with your physical eye. I therefore give you the power of divine vision. Behold My power as the Lord of all."
-BHAGAVAD GITA, CHAPTER 11, VERSE 8

Mother continued, "You may have a longing to realize God, but it may not last long, because the intensity will weaken, unless you are a very competent student. Your longing will come and go, it will be very unstable. Even if you are able to sustain your longing, you may still have an intense craving to enjoy the pleasures of the world. You don't know how to create a balance between the inner and the outer worlds. If the Master is not there to guide you from time to time, you may stray away from the path, you may journey in the wrong direction, or, you may stop in the middle of your journey and fall back into the world. You will then lose all your faith and think that there is no such state as God- or Self-Realization.

"Attachment to the Master's external form is like the *gopis'* attachment to Krishna's form, or Hanuman's attachment to Rama's form, or the attachment that the disciples of Buddha and Jesus had towards them. Those disciples lived with God. To live in the physical presence of a true Master, and to be attached to his external form, is like living with and being attached to Pure Consciousness, or the Supreme. It inspires you and creates an intense longing within you, and you will then be able to sustain that intensity. When you are under the watchful eye of the Master, you cannot stray away from the path, provided that you live in faith, surrender and obedience to the Master's words.

"Being attached to the external form of a Satguru is like having direct contact with the Supreme Truth. The presence of such a Great Being is so filled with Divinity that you feel it in your heart, you see it with your eyes and you sense it everywhere. It is a tangible sensation that you experience through the Master's entire being - when you look into his eyes, when you feel his touch, observe his actions and listen to his words.

"Everyone wants someone to be attached to; a boyfriend or a girlfriend, a husband or a wife. Children cling to their parents or their toys, or they demand the company of their brothers and sisters, and people want friends. There are countless things in the world to keep the human mind busy. Companies and businessmen are constantly producing new products for this purpose. In their search for happiness (that is, in their need to quiet their minds) people run from one object to another. But they soon find the object boring and are then compelled to run after a new one. The search is never-ending.

"When there is something new on the market, when, for example, a new movie is released, your mind becomes excited and you want to see it. The more you hear about the movie, the more you want to see it. And when your desire has been fulfilled, the nagging mind quiets down for a while until you hear about another movie, or something else. This is the nature of the mind. It cannot be silent, it cannot be alone by itself and be happy. If it has nothing to attach itself to, you become extremely restless. The mind creates a long chain of attachments. People live in a fantasy world and are building castles in the air. If they cannot dream, or if they have nothing to think about, they may go crazy or commit suicide.

"You are bound to become bored with all the objects and experiences that you get in the world. You can never remain with anything for any length of time. You have to move on, because the mind is constantly moving from one thing to another; it forces you to jump from one thing to another. Boredom is bound to occur in every single worldly situation, because of the incessant demands of the mind. This is why people in the West try different boyfriends and girlfriends, or husbands and wives, or a new house in a different city. They want to try new things, new relationships, because they easily get tired of the old and familiar. The mind is attached to a thousand different things and it is pulling you in all directions.

"As the mind is always vacillating and is full of negativity, even the spiritual longing that you are experiencing now may disappear, because your present longing for realization stems from the mind. One day you may suddenly get bored, because it is the nature of the mind to be bored with everything, and because it is always wanting something new. If you have nothing to hold on to or relate to, it is bound to get bored with spiritual life as well.

"In order to steady your mind and make it still, you need to be attached to something higher than the mind. The mind is the noisiest place in the world. Unless there is something on which it can really contemplate or meditate, the mind will not be quiet. But the object of one's meditation or contemplation should not be anything familiar, for then the mind will soon get bored.

"The longing that you have now for God-Realization may be just one attachment among many. You cannot withstand strong temptations for any length of time. In your present mental state, your other attachments are much stronger than your attachment to God-Realization. The longing that you feel could stem from some excitement and attraction which you might have felt during a particularly inspiring moment. It could die away soon, because boredom is bound to occur if you don't feel a much more powerful and tempting pull. That pull is your attachment to the Master's external form. It is that attachment which balances out all other attachments. By being attracted and attached to the Master's form you develop a special power to withstand all other attractions. The Master's physical presence is pervaded with Divinity, so there is no chance for boredom, because boredom happens only when the mind is concerned with the objects, experiences and ideas of the world. The mind gets easily bored with external things, because true happiness is not the nature of anything which belongs to the world. A Satguru, however, is the very source of eternal bliss and happiness. His very being is immortal, and if one is inquisitive enough, one can, in his presence, behold infinity unfolding in infinite ways. Boredom is therefore very rare in the Master's presence. He is the embodiment of the Divine; and boredom cannot happen if one is receptive to his presence which is Divine. Attachment to the Master's physical form fills the disciple's heart with love, enthusiasm, contentment and a feeling of freshness. The Master himself will instill these qualities in the disciple. Whenever the disciple feels depressed and discouraged, the Master, through his unconditional love and compassion, or by giving the disciple an inspiring experience, lifts him out of his negative condition and encourages him to march forward with new determination and enthusiasm. This helps to steady the disciple's noisy mind and make it still, because the presence of a true Master is the only place where the restless mind can rest forever without getting bored.

"Spirituality is not an observable fact, like the sun and the moon, the mountains and rivers. Spirituality is faith. Only complete, undivided faith can help one reach the goal.

"Every human being in the world is either intellectual or emotional. It is difficult for intellectuals to believe, because they only believe in visible things. Since God is invisible, to believe in His existence one has to depend solely on faith, and faith is not an intellectual process. Even though emotionally centered people may believe more easily, it is not easy for them to believe completely either, because their faith is not undivided; their faith is only partial because of their doubting minds. And soon, when they begin to get bored, they will look for another object to pin their faith upon.

"Both intellectual and emotional people need evidence of something solid and visible in order to believe and to strengthen their faith. Otherwise, they may develop a little bit of interest, a little longing to realize God, and then after a short time, if they don't get any real experience or feel a tangible presence of the Divine, they may turn back and say, 'This is just nonsense. There is no such thing as God or God-Realization.' Of course, the problem lies within their own mind and in their lack of patience, but still, if they have something which they can relate to, they will feel assured and inspired. That will help them remain in spiritual life and to live according to its principles. But this is possible only in the presence of a true Master, by developing a personal relationship with him, and by creating an attachment to his external form. By doing this you are establishing a relationship with God, the Supreme Consciousness, your own inner Self. This is not like developing attachment to an ordinary individual; it is a relationship which will help you to be detached in all circumstances. It prepares your mind to take the final leap into God-Consciousness."

Silence fell upon the listeners. Mother's powerful words seemed to be resounding everywhere, within the hearts of those who were listening and outside in the physical environment as well. An inspiring meditative atmosphere prevailed, as if to give a tangible experience of what Mother was talking about - the significance of a great *Mahatma's* physical presence, the importance of feeling attached to Her external form, and the necessity of having a relationship with the physical embodiment of the Divine.

CHAPTER SIXTEEN

MOTHER, LIBERATOR OF THE SOUL

*M*other was sitting with some of the residents and a few devotees in the coconut grove in front of the temple. Mother was talking about different subjects with the householder devotees. Suddenly Mother turned towards Balu and said, "Ottoormon (My son, Ottoor) wishes to see Amma. Bring him here." Balu got up and went to fetch Ottoor. Ottoor was staying in a room especially built for him, above the underground meditation cells, situated just behind the old temple.

Ottoor Unni Nambootiripadu was a well-known poet and Sanskrit scholar in Kerala. He was an authority on the *Srimad Bhagavatam*, which mainly depicts the *Avatars* of Vishnu, especially that of Lord Krishna and His childhood sports. Ottoor's beautiful poems glorifying Krishna are famous throughout India, and Krishna devotees love them very much. As an exponent of the *Srimad Bhagavatam* and also as a gifted poet and author, Ottoor had won many titles and awards, both from the central and state governments. He was a great devotee of Lord Krishna and was closely associated with the famous Guruvayoor temple of Kerala. The following song, *Kannante Punya*, will help the reader get an idea about the blessed poet's wonderful compositions and his devotion.

> *When will I hear*
> *the auspicious names of Kanna*
> *sounding in my ears?*
> *And upon hearing them*
> *when will my hair stand on end*
> *and when will I be totally*
> *immersed in tears?*
>
> *Being immersed in tears*
> *when will I become pure?*
> *And in that state of absolute purity*
> *when will I sing His Names*
> *spontaneously?*
>
> *And as I sing in ecstasy*
> *when will I forget the earth and the sky?*
> *And forgetting everything*
> *when will I dance*
> *in utter devotion?*
> *And as I dance, will my steps*
> *sweep the stains*
> *from the stage of the world?*
>
> *In that playful dance*
> *in which I sweep all stains away*
> *I will cry out loud*

And through that cry,
will my purity be sent
in the eight directions?

And when the play has been enacted
when will I fall at last
into my Mother's lap?
And lying on my Mother's lap
when will I sleep blissfully?

As I sleep
when will I dream
of the beautiful form of Sri Krishna
who dwells within my heart?
And as I wake up
when will I see Sri Krishna
the Enchanter of the world?

This song was written by the great poet twenty-five years before the Holy Mother's incarnation on earth. There is a most touching and wonderful story behind this song. It shows how an incarnation of God fulfills the sincere and wholehearted prayers of a true devotee. In this poem he says, "And when the play has been enacted, when will I fall at last, into my Mother's lap? And lying on my Mother's lap, when will I sleep blissfully?"

Ottoor first met Mother in 1983. He had been invited to Mother's 30th birthday celebration. Ottoor had heard about Mother from one of Her devotees while he was visiting Trivandrum. He immediately felt an intense, spontaneous desire to meet Her. Ottoor strongly felt that Mother was the divine incarnation of the Supreme Goddess and also of Lord Krishna, his beloved deity. Thus, he came to meet Mother on Her birthday, on September 27, 1983. And once he had met Mother, Ottoor, the eighty-five year old devotee, poet and scholar, became like a two year old child who constantly craved the care and attention of his Mother. He realized that he had at long last reached his destiny and decided to spend the rest of his life in Mother's presence. From then on, he also began to compose poems to Mother. The relationship between Mother and the eighty-five year old poet was unique - something very special and extraordinarily beautiful. Mother greatly appreciated his childlike nature, and She gave him the pet name, 'Unni Kanna' (baby Krishna).

Just like a child, he used to ask Mother before he did anything. If he wanted to take a special medicine, he would get Mother's permission before taking it. Even before he would use a different bath soap or change his diet, he would first ask for Mother's permission. Only if Mother said yes would he do it. Otherwise, he never did anything different. Sometimes he wanted Mother to feed him. At other times he wished to lie on Her lap. The occasions were not rare, when one could hear him calling loudly from his room, "Amma! Amma!" at the top of his voice. He did this whenever he had a strong urge to see Her. At such times, if Mother happened to be in the vicinity, She would go to see him in his room. If Mother was in Her room and not nearby, She would send him some *prasad* through Gayatri or another messenger. Being aware of his childlike nature, Mother sometimes sent somebody to bring him to the hut when She was giving *darshan* to the devotees. She then showered him with great love and affection and let him sit very close to Her. During those moments, Ottoor, who was always complaining about the state of his body, forgot about his suffering. He always loved to sit close to Mother. Ottoor often used to say, "I get so much energy when I sit next to Mother."

This rare Mother-child relationship is beyond the human intellect. The eighty-five year old renowned poet calling Mother, who was only thirty years old at the time, "Amma", is perhaps difficult for the human mind to understand. How can the intellect comprehend such a mystery? For Ottoor Unni Nambootiripadu, Mother was both his Guru and God. In Mother he saw both Lord Krishna, his beloved deity, and the Mother of the Universe. This was clearly depicted in all his compositions to Mother, including the one hundred eight Names of Mother which were written by him. The following is a song about Mother, written by Ottoor.

> *O Mother*
> *You are the embodiment of both Krishna and Kali.*
> *O Mother*

You sanctify the worlds with Your smile
and Your song,
with Your glance, Your touch and Your dance,
with Your delightful talk,
by the touch of Your Holy Feet,
and by the nectar of Your Love.

O Mother
Who is the celestial creeper
joyously and bounteously
bestowing all the purusharthas
from dharma *to* moksha,
to all sentient and insentient beings
from Lord Brahma down to a blade of grass.

O Mother
Who astonishes the three worlds,
inundating all human beings
and the bees and the birds,
the worms and the trees
by the turbulent waves of Your love.

Ottoor had only one wish. Whenever he received Mother's *darshan*, his only prayer to Her was, "Amma, when I breathe my last, let my head rest on Your lap. This is my only wish, my only prayer. O my Mother, please let me die with my head on Your lap." This prayer was repeated fervently to Mother whenever he met Her. The poet chanted his prayer so much that his wish became known to practically all of Mother's devotees and to his own admirers.

Soon after Ottoor met Mother he became a permanent resident at the Ashram. He had a very blissful, contented stay at the Ashram. He always used to say, "Now I know that God has not abandoned me, because I am living in His presence and I am basking in His divine love. I used to feel greatly disappointed when I thought of the fact that I couldn't be with Krishna or Chaitanya Mahaprabhu,[16] or any of the *Mahatmas*. But I don't feel that anymore, because I believe that Mother is all of them."

Just before Mother's third world tour in 1989, Ottoor's health took a very bad turn. His body was falling apart, and even though Mother made all the necessary arrangements for his treatment, Ottoor was unable to regain his health. He became very weak and his eyesight was failing rapidly. Unable to see properly, he could not write poems the way he used to, instead he dictated them to his nephew, Narayanan, who also took care of Ottoor's personal needs.

Though Ottoor's physical condition grew worse, his childlike innocence and his attitude towards Mother did not change at all. In fact, it became even more intense. His well-known prayer to be allowed to die in Mother's lap became constant. When his eye sight became very poor, Ottoor said to Mother, "It's okay if Amma wants to take away my external sight. But, O

---

[16] 1485-1535

Divine Mother of the heavens, kindly bless Your servant by removing the inner darkness and open the inner eye. Please don't refuse the prayer of this child."

To this Mother lovingly replied, "Unni Kanna, don't worry! It will definitely happen. How can Amma refuse Your innocent prayer?"

Just a week before Mother left for Her third world tour, Ottoor's health suddenly deteriorated. His condition became very serious and he was completely bedridden. Everybody thought he was going to die. Ottoor was not afraid of death. His only fear was that he would die when Mother was abroad. He expressed this fear to Mother and said, "Amma, I know that You are everywhere and that Your lap is as big as the universe. Still, I pray for You to be physically present when I leave my body. If I die while You are away, my wish to die in Your lap will not be fulfilled." Mother caressed him affectionately and replied with great authority, "No, my son, Unni Kanna, that will not happen! You can be sure that you will leave your body only after Amma's return." This was a great consolation to Ottoor. As this assurance came directly from Mother's own lips, Ottoor firmly believed that death couldn't touch him before Mother came back.

After three months of touring around the world, Mother returned to the Ashram in August. During Her absence, Ottoor had been undergoing treatment in the home of an ayurvedic doctor, who was also an ardent devotee of Mother. He took very good care of the poet, and Ottoor's health improved a little, but after a short time he again became worse. Mother then told Ottoor to return to the Ashram, as the time for him to leave his body was getting close.

During Krishna's birthday, Ottoor sat near Mother and participated in all the celebrations which took place. The day after Krishna's birthday was a Devi Bhava day. The Bhava *darshan* ended at two-thirty in the morning, after which Mother went to Ottoor's room. He was very weak but was extremely happy to see Mother. The great poet wept like a child and prayed to Mother, "O Amma, Mother of the Universe, please call me back! Please call me back, quickly!" Just like a mother caring for her child, Mother rubbed and soothed the poet's chest and forehead, and She caressed his head with overflowing love and compassion.

A devotee had offered Mother a new silk mattress that day. She now asked Bri. Gayatri to bring the mattress to Ottoor's room. Gayatri left and soon returned carrying the mattress. Mother picked up Ottoor's thin, frail body from the bed, and like a mother carrying a baby in her arms, Mother held Ottoor in Her arms, while Gayatri, Balu and Narayanan spread the new mattress on the cot. As Ottoor was experiencing this demonstration of Mother's infinite compassion, he cried out, "O Amma, Mother of the Universe, why are You showering so much love and compassion upon this unworthy child?

Oh Amma, Amma, Amma..."

Mother lay him gently down on the cot and said, "Unni Kanna, my son, sleep well. Mother will come in the morning."

"O Amma, put me to eternal sleep," replied Ottoor.

Mother once again glanced lovingly at Ottoor before She left the room.

That night, the poet dictated one last song.

> *Treating me and hoping for a cure*
> *the physicians admitted their defeat.*
> *All my relatives have turned despondent.*
> *O Mother, lay me on Your lap with tender love*
> *Save me and never forsake me.*
>
> *O Saradamani, O Sudhamani, O Holy Mother*
> *Lay me fondly in Your tender lap*
> *Reveal the moon of Ambadi on Your face*
> *Tarry not to bless me with immortality.*
>
> *Reveal Uncle Moon, Nanda's son*
> *on Your sweet face*
> *and lay this little Kanna on Your lap.*
> *O Mother, lull him to sleep.*

At seven the next morning, Friday the 25th of August 1989, Mother sent for Narayanan. When he arrived, She told him that Ottoor was going to leave his body in a few hours. Mother further told Narayanan to find out from his uncle whether he wanted his mortal frame to be buried at the Ashram or at his birth place. Narayanan went back to the room and conveyed to his uncle what Mother had said. Though his voice was very feeble, Ottoor clearly replied as he gestured emphatically with his hand, "I will be buried here, in this sacred land. There is nowhere else."

At about ten o'clock Ottoor asked Bri. Leela,[17] who was standing by his side, to call Mother. But Leela didn't pay much attention to Ottoor's request; she was holding some medicine in her hands and was explaining the dosage to Narayanan. Finally, Ottoor gave Leela a hard push and gestured, "No more medicine! Go and get Mother!" Leela then left the room, and for the next few minutes one could clearly see Ottoor's lips moving as he constantly chanted, "Amma, Amma, Amma..." During this chanting Ottoor went into a *samadhi* like state.

At this time Mother was in Her room. As Leela came in through the door, Mother said to both Gayatri and Leela, "In a few minutes, Ottoormon is going to leave his body. But it is not yet time for Amma to be there. Now, his mind is completely focused on Amma. This intense thought will culminate in a state of *layana* (merging). When this happens, Amma will go to him. The intensity would be reduced if Amma had gone to him earlier." A few seconds later, Mother left Her room and

---

[17] Bri. Leela is today known as Swamini Atmaprana. She was previously a practising medical doctor.

went over to Ottoor's room, followed by Leela. Mother entered Ottoor's room with a beaming smile and sat down on the bed close to Ottoor. With an extraordinary glow on Her face, She kept gazing at Her Unni Kanna's face, as if telling him, "Come, my son! My darling Unni Kanna, come and merge in Me, your eternal Mother." As Mother had predicted earlier, in Her room, Ottoor was lying in a state of *layana*. Mother caressed him, rubbing his head and chest with overflowing love and compassion. Even though Ottoor was in a state of *samadhi*, his eyes remained half open. There was no sign of any pain or struggle on his face. One could easily see how absorbed and blissful he was. Mother slowly moved closer to his head. She gently lifted his head up and placed it on Her lap. And as Mother held Her darling son's head in Her lap, She held Her right hand on His chest, and She continued to gaze at his face.

As the great poet devotee, Mother's Unni Kanna, lay on Her lap, Mother gently caressed his eyelids, and they were closed forever. Ottoor left his body and his soul merged with Mother for all eternity. Mother bent down and placed a loving, affectionate kiss on his forehead.

Thus, the last line of his own composition, *Kannante Punya,* which he had written twenty-five years before Mother's incarnation, was fulfilled by the all-compassionate Mother of the Universe: *And when the play has been enacted, when will I fall at last into my Mother's lap? And lying on my Mother's lap, when will I sleep blissfully? As I sleep, when will I dream of the beautiful form of Sri Krishna who dwells within my heart? And as I wake up, when will I see Sri Krishna, the Enchanter of the world?*

This incident stands as a great example of how the *Satguru*, who is none other than God Himself, fulfills the desires of a sincere devotee.

Another significant point in this incident is Mother's response when Ottoor expressed his fear that he might leave his body while Mother was away on the world tour. To this She had responded, as has already been mentioned, "No, my son, Unni Kanna, that will not happen! You can be sure that you will leave your body only after Amma's return."

Who can give such an assurance, guaranteeing that a person will not die before a certain period of time? Mother's reply sounds so categorical. It is as if death is perfectly under Her control as She says, "Unless I permit it, you cannot touch my darling child." And death obeyed Her! Who else can command death like this but Amma, who according to Ottoor is "the Divine Mother of the Universe, who is the complete manifestation of the Absolute Truth (Brahman); who is existence, knowledge and bliss embodied; who verily is the Supreme Goddess in human form...?"[18] Who, but God

---

[18] From the one hundred eight Names.

alone, can issue such an order? It is only the One who has gone beyond Death who can say, "Stop, and wait until I tell you when." Isn't this what happened here?

After Ottoor's death, N.V. Krishna Warrier, a famous writer, linguist and scholar of Kerala, wrote an editorial about Ottoor in a major newspaper. "Ottoor saw the Universal Mother in the young Mata Amritanandamayi. She endearingly loved the aged Ottoor like her own son. It was indeed a unique Mother-son relationship."

Let us now go back to that afternoon, a few years before Ottoor left his body. Balu returned to the coconut grove with Ottoor, holding the old poet by his hand. With great devotion and humility Ottoor fell at Mother's feet. As he lay prostrate in front of Mother he said, "Amma, You knew that this servant wanted to see You. I was longing to be with You. O Amma, You sent for me because You knew the wish of my heart. Amma, kindly place Your holy feet on my head." Mother laughed and said, "Unni Kanna, no, no! They are all full of dirt." Ottoor, in a very powerful and august voice said, "What are you saying? Dirty! Your feet? O Amma, do not say that! I know that the dust of Your feet is sufficient to kill the darkness of ignorance in the whole world. Please place Your feet on my head, otherwise I won't get up."

Finally, Mother had to yield to Ottoor's wish and She placed Her feet on his head. Ottoor, the great devotee, was thrilled. He repeated loudly, *"Anandoham, Dhanyoham, Anandoham"* (Blissful am I, blessed am I, blissful am I). And as he was chanting, he took the dust of Mother's feet and rubbed it all over his body.

Ottoor knelt in front of Mother and She embraced him affectionately. The great poet looked up at Her like an innocent child, and with eyes filled with tears he said, "O Amma, never abandon this child. Let me always be in Your divine presence."

GLOSSARY

ABHAYA MUDRA: Hand pose indicating bestowal of fearlessness.

ACHARA: Customary observances.

ARATI: Vespers, waving the burning camphor, which leaves no residue, with ringing of bells at the end of worship, representing the complete offering of the ego to God.

ATMA SHAKTI: Energy of the Self or Soul.

AVATAR: Incarnation of God.

BHAJAN: Devotional singing.

DARSHAN: Audience of a holy person or deity.

DHARMA: Righteousness, in accordance with Divine Harmony.

JAGRAT: Waking state.

KIRTAN: Singing.

LALITA ASHTHOTTARA: One hundred and eight Names of the Divine Mother Sri Lalita.

LAYANA: Merger into God-Consciousness.

LEELA: A divine play or show, appearance.

MAHATMA: Great Soul or Sage.

MAYA: Illusion.

MOKSHA: Release from the cycle of birth and death.

MUDRA: Hand pose indicative of mystic truths.

NIRVANA: Liberation from the cycle of birth and death.

PADA PUJA: Worship of the feet of God or a saint.

PANCHAMRITAM: A sweet jam-like substance offering to God in Hindu temples.

PARASHAKTI: The Supreme Energy or Goddess.

PEETHAM: The holy seat on which Mother sits during Devi Bhava.

PRALAYAGNI: The fire of Universal Dissolution at the end of creation.

PRASAD: Consecrated offerings distributed at the end of worship.

PUJA: Ritualistic worship.

PUNYA: Merit, opposite of sin.

PURNAM: Full or perfect.

PURUSHA: Male being, the Spirit or God.

PURUSHARTHAS: The four goals or ends of human existence, i.e. wealth, enjoyment, righteousness, and Liberation.

RAJAS: One of the three gunas or qualities of Nature, the principle of activity.

SADHAK: A spiritual aspirant.

SADHANA: Spiritual practice.

SAKSHI BHAVA: The attitude of being a witness.

SAMADHI: Absorption of the mind into Reality or Truth.

SANKALPA: A resolve.

SANNYASIN: One who has taken formal vows of renunciation.

SARVASAKSHI: All-witness.

SATTVIC: One of the three gunas of Nature, the principle of purity and serenity.

SHIVA LINGAM: The emblem of Lord Shiva, oval in shape.

SUSHUPTHI: The state of deep, dreamless sleep.

SWAPNA: Dream.

TAPAS: Austerity, hardship undergone for the sake of self-purification.

UPANISHADS: The concluding portion of the Vedas or scriptures of the Hindus, dealing with the nature of the Absolute Brahman, the Transcendent Reality, the True Self.

UTSAVAM: Festival.

VAHANA: Vehicle or mount.

VASANAS: Residual impressions of objects and actions experienced, habits.

VEDAS: The authoritative scriptures of the Hindus, lit. "Knowledge."

YANTRA: Mystic diagram.

Index